SOUL
TRADER

PRAISE FOR...

Rasheed is grounded, energizing and hugely inspirational – as is this book which is insightful for those dreaming of a business and those already running one.

Clare Longrigg, Deputy Editor, *Psychologies*

Rasheed has written a book that I hope inspires a whole new generation of heart-centred entrepreneurs who will care about the people and the planet not just profit.

Rachel Elnaugh, award-winning entrepreneur, business mentor and star of BBC's *Dragons' Den* seasons 1 and 2

If you have picked up this book don't put it down until you've read it because it contains chapter after chapter of relevant and essential information which will benefit you for the rest of your life. It is not just a business tool, it is a life tool that you are holding. The words are written by a man who actually cares what happens to you now, and for the rest of your life. A brilliant and motivational book by a knowledgeable, intelligent and thoughtful author.

Stephen Fear, Entrepreneur in Residence, British Library

SOUL
TRADER

Putting the heart back
into your business

RASHEED OGUNLARU

KoganPage

LONDON PHILADELPHIA NEW DELHI

Publisher's note
Every possible effort has been made to ensure that the information contained in this book is accurate at the time of going to press, and the publishers and author cannot accept responsibility for any errors or omissions, however caused. No responsibility for loss or damage occasioned to any person acting, or refraining from action, as a result of the material in this publication can be accepted by the editor, the publisher or the author.

First published in Great Britain and the United States in 2012 by Kogan Page Limited

Apart from any fair dealing for the purposes of research or private study, or criticism or review, as permitted under the Copyright, Designs and Patents Act 1988, this publication may only be reproduced, stored or transmitted, in any form or by any means, with the prior permission in writing of the publishers, or in the case of reprographic reproduction in accordance with the terms and licences issued by the CLA. Enquiries concerning reproduction outside these terms should be sent to the publishers at the undermentioned addresses:

120 Pentonville Road	1518 Walnut Street, Suite 1100	4737/23 Ansari Road
London N1 9JN	Philadelphia PA 19102	Daryaganj
United Kingdom	USA	New Delhi 110002
www.koganpage.com		India

© Rasheed Ogunlaru, 2012

The right of Rasheed Ogunlaru to be identified as the author of this work has been asserted by him in accordance with the Copyright, Designs and Patents Act 1988.

ISBN   978 0 7494 6637 4
E-ISBN   978 0 7494 6638 1

British Library Cataloguing-in-Publication Data

A CIP record for this book is available from the British Library.

Library of Congress Cataloging-in-Publication Data

Ogunlaru, Rasheed, 1970-
   Soul trader : putting the heart back into your business / Rasheed Ogunlaru.
     p. cm.
   ISBN 978-0-7494-6637-4 – ISBN 978-0-7494-6638-1 (ebook) 1. Success in business. 2. Entrepreneurship. 3. Customer relations. 4. Management. I. Title.
   HF5386.O376 2012
   658–dc23
                                                                    2012013050

Typeset by Graphicraft Limited, Hong Kong
Printed and bound in India by Replika Press Pvt Ltd

CONTENTS

6 Creativity: The magic mix of inspiration and action   163

7 Compassion: How to truly take care of business   211

8   Change: How to face, shape and embrace it 231

ABOUT THE AUTHOR

Rasheed Ogunlaru
is a leading life coach, motivational speaker and business/corporate coach. His career spans over 16 years in coaching, training, media and performance. His clients include entertainers, entrepreneurs, chief executives, teachers, healers, high achievers, organizations and the public. He appears regularly in the media on life, work, relationship and business issues, including appear-

ances on the BBC and ITV News. He is an inspiring and empowering public speaker, uniquely popular across the business, spiritual and personal development circuits. He is a qualified member of the Coaching Academy and is former Co-Director of Samaritans (Central London). He is co-author of an inspiring range of books and downloads, including *Soul Trader* and *Become Who You Are*. He is the business coach partner of the British Library's Business and IP Centre, where he runs the inspiring Your Life, Your Business workshop. Rasheed is also the coach to TiE UK's mentoring programme.

Prior to his career in coaching Rasheed enjoyed success as a communications manager and media trainer, a career which began at 18 when he worked for *Which?*, where he became a press officer, media trainer and media spokesperson. After 10 years he moved on to a career as a singer–performer. On meeting countless performers who struggled with their confidence and careers he retrained as a coach to help people take charge of their lives. Today his unique 'Become who you are' approach enables people of all backgrounds to achieve greater fulfilment in all areas of their lives and careers – from within. He is widely considered a leading specialist on inner fulfilment.

For further information on Rasheed's work, or to enjoy other titles, visit his website **www.rasaru.com.**

www.twitter.com/rasheedogunlaru
www.youtube.com/ogunlaru

PREFACE

I remember heading to the British Library to run my monthly workshop for entrepreneurs. I wondered how I'd begin it this time. It came to me. I arrived and said:

> There will be two workshops going on in this room at the same time today: one for your head and one for your heart. Your head wants to know: How am I going to make this business work? I hoped there'd be refreshments. Did I leave the window open at home? Are we going to finish on time? I'd better remember to call so and so... And then there's your heart; your heart wants to just be yourself. In a way it wants nothing: just to be. It just wants to do what's most true to you.

Everyone in the room nodded, agreed, gently smiled to themselves or silently acknowledged. I have said the same or similar words at almost every talk I have given for several years. I have said those similar words to thousands of people in different venues at different events, and the reaction has always been the same.

We know it to be true, but too often lose that balance and that inner wisdom. If your heart isn't in it, why are you? Both head *and* heart will be necessary for the journey, for running your business. This book will help bring them together, perhaps for the first time.

When your head and heart work together, magic happens. Your heart is able to be and feel fulfilled. And your head is able to do its job: to plan, prepare, figure things out and try its best to keep you safe and secure.

With head and heart together you double your odds of true success, and that nagging inner doubt dissolves, for at last your head and your heart are both heard. There is no inner conflict. The journey can be rewarding, fulfilling, enjoyable and heart-warming. When challenges come you will have the heart to face them. When opportunities come you will embrace them with a sound mind and good heart. Your life will not be an afterthought. It will be dear to your heart throughout.

Welcome to the world of the soul trader.

ACKNOWLEDGEMENTS

I would like to thank everyone who has played a part in my journey from head to heart throughout my life and career. I am grateful to my family and friends, my colleagues in all my jobs and all the singers and creatives I have heard, seen, met and been inspired by. I'm grateful to those with whom I spoke and volunteered in my time at Samaritans. I'm grateful to all the clients I've worked with and all my contacts and associates – and everyone who has come along to my talks. Thanks to those who've read my writing and watched or listened to my talks or videos, whom I may never have met. I'd also like to thank the wonderful team at the British Library and TiE UK, where I'm delighted to work with new and established owners.

I am thankful to Liz and the team at Kogan Page and for the serendipitous way in which this book came to life. I'm thankful to all the clients, contacts and delegates I have met and worked with as a coach and speaker.

Everything and everyone has played a remarkable part, and I am deeply grateful. This and every experience has made me rich beyond words, possessions or status.

I would particularly like to thank my mother, who could have gone into business herself in the world of fashion. In many ways the gifts I share here have sprung from the magical gifts of clarity, courage and compassion she instilled in me.

Thank you all.

There are many books out there for your head. This one is dedicated to your heart.

INTRODUCTION

Most people do not go into business solely to make money. They want to make a living, make an impact, make a contribution, make a statement, make something of real worth and value. They want to enjoy what they do, and make themselves happy and their families secure and proud. They want to make a break from the humdrum, and express their skills and abilities. But sooner or later many business owners fall into the same old trap, lose sight of what's important and struggle with life balance.

At the same time the world – and business world – is changing. The marketplace is more crowded and noisy than ever. We're overwhelmed, and tired and numb with being 'sold to'. We eventually leave the job where we were merely a cog in the wheel of the workplace, and avoid and resent the businesses for which we're just cash in the till. We leave because they don't care about us, it doesn't serve us any more, and our heart isn't in it.

We have a heightened sense of consciousness, not only of the kind of life balance that we want, but also the kind of business we want to set up or work for. We are more concerned about businesses ethically and equitably, as well as about their history and reliability. We want to know how our goods are sourced, resourced and supplied. We want to know if a business is actually sound, will do a good job and will take care of our interests – not just its own.

Soul traders follow their own paths and their hearts. They run the kind of businesses that they would actually love to buy from and work in. They want to build businesses on their own values that serve you, your customers, your lifestyle and your wider concerns.

The seven principles in this book will help you do just that – to establish a business that is enriching and enjoyable personally and professionally.

It is a new era, the era of the soul trader: it is about business with an open heart – with you *and* others in mind.

About the soul trader

Soul traders are people who want to run a business that they are truly passionate about. They care about their customers and those they do business with. They often operate in a field – or undertake a cause – that's close to their heart. Some run traditional businesses and wish to bring their own unique spin to it or to improve or revolutionize it. Many are people from all walks of life who wish to do what they love for a living. Soul traders also include inventors, healers, innovators, teachers, leaders, carers, artists, entertainers, ethical entrepreneurs, environmentalists, creatives, mentors and therapists. Some soul traders are all these things – and are mavericks.

Overall, soul traders want to run a business that sits with the values and ethics that sit with them and their lifestyle. Sometimes they are tired and stressed by the old ways of doing things and need to bring more life balance, fun and creativity to what they do and to their lives – or simply seek fresh inspiration. Some soul traders are consciously or unconsciously on a journey of self-discovery.

Some have been in employment their whole lives; some have been in business for most of theirs. Some 'choose' this path, and some find that life events have led them here. Some feel compelled to be their own boss; some feel they've had no choice; others feel they choose their path. Some know exactly where they are going and are drawn to this book, as it resonates deeply with them, and others are looking to find their path – or a new one – and will find this useful guidance. Most wish to shape or embrace their path and destiny. Many soul traders have a number of facets to their lives and wish to run a business that sits well and supports their family, social and personal priorities, and passions.

Soul traders are sometimes even visionaries who are interested not only in enriching their lives and those of their loved ones but in leaving the world richer than they found it. Welcome, one and all.

Book overview: you are the key

This book helps you in two ways: you'll gain deeper insight, inspiration and creativity; and you'll become more focused, strategic, productive and effective. Both aspects will be necessary along your journey.

On the one hand the chapters work sequentially and build on one another. They will help develop your business – whatever its stage. So starting with **clarity** you will become clear about where you are, what you want from your life and business, and how you can set or fine-tune your goals and identify your next steps. Then you will start on a journey of understanding your **customers** and developing **courage** to seek and win business through the right blend of **co-operation** and **conversations**. This is not the whole journey; staying on track is tough, and developing and sustaining a business that you, customers and others love will require the **creativity** to balance and manage your life and business, as well as genuine, rich relationships and **compassion**. The concluding chapter on **change** will help support you as you and your business develop and face transition – as you will throughout.

That said, some themes and chapters may jump out at you as being especially relevant to where you are, and you may wish to focus on them first and read them in a different order. The chapters have a rich crossover. You'll see elements of one in another; the messages are often reinforced to help and remind you to identify, extract and utilize what's relevant for you. You'll probably find that starting at the top and following the book through on the first reading is most useful, and then you can dip in and out to revisit chapters as they are appropriate for you, your business and your circumstances.

Ultimately you are the key. You are the captain of the ship. This book and the chapters will prompt, probe, energize and illuminate you along your path. Your openness to it, and your ability to interpret and apply it as it relates to you and as it resonates with you, is where the magic of this book really comes to life.

Chapter guide

Clarity

This opening chapter will help you first to develop *insight*. You will need to be clear on who you are, what you want and what you are about.

Then you will need *foresight*: to develop or clarify your vision and mission and to set the path ahead – and to begin to see and discover what makes you unique to others in the market.

Finally and crucially this chapter will help you to *stay clear*: to keep space for yourself, planning and development. It will help you foster *awareness* of what is important and to adjust to – and sometimes avoid – some of life's and business's changes and challenges.

Look at this chapter whenever you need to remember, reconnect, reconsider, review and reset your goals. ♥ ♥ ♥

Customers

Your own perspective and wishes are not enough; business is all about serving your customers and marketplace. This second chapter helps you to understand the types, desires, drivers, fears and needs of your (potential) customers so that you can find, connect to, serve and keep them.

Together with clarity it provides the base for the rest of the book and your journey.

This chapter also reminds you to keep your customers in sight and mind and in your heart, to develop a strong, sustainable business that your customers love and will tell others about.

Visit this chapter when you are starting, diversifying, or developing products and services, or when you are keen to or need to enter new markets – and to engage and relate to present or potential customers. ♥ ♥ ♥

Courage

Business is a journey that will include degrees of challenge, competition, change, conflicting demands and uncertainty. It is not for the faint-hearted.

This chapter will help you discover your *inner strength*, *courage* and *inspiration* to help carry you through. By tapping into your courage and staying true to your heart, the challenges and experience that you gather will help you arrive at deeper wisdom and even more powerful ways of serving your customers. ♥ ♥ ♥

Cooperation

Everything is *interrelated*, *interdependent* and ultimately *one*. What's more, you will need specific help, support, suppliers, staff and contacts to establish, run and grow your business, sales and profits. This chapter will help you to tap into your existing *networks* and to extend them to access and create new opportunities that will profit you, your customers and others.

Revisit this chapter whenever you are stuck, frustrated or encountering challenges – and when you wish to extend and strengthen your business or network. ♥ ♥ ♥

Conversations

Customer conversion relies on the right customer *conversation*. The right word will open the door, and the wrong one will slam it shut in your face.

This essential chapter will help you have rich conversations leading to rich relationships and rewards. It will help you establish, sustain and develop strong relationships and business – and let them pass when necessary.

Consult this chapter when you need to pitch, present, persuade or promote. It will help you warmly approach and address customers and suppliers – and indeed family, friends and supporters. ♥ ♥ ♥

Creativity

Business is all about *creativity, inventiveness* and *adventure*. But so often soul traders forget this. This chapter helps remind you of your magic. It helps you explore what works for you and how it is that you work at your best in order that you become more effective, excited, exciting and engaging.

Play with this chapter when you need *focus*, to get organized and productive – or when you need to bring *fun, freedom, balance* and *flexibility* into your life and business. ♥ ♥ ♥

Compassion

Love you, love what you do and love others too is the mantra of this chapter.

Compassion and its source *love* are words that are not often used in business, but they are the qualities that will elevate you from running a business on stress, fear, sweat and tears to one that is flowing from a place of openness and possibility.

Visit this chapter if you are lost, overwhelmed or burnt out and when nothing seems to work. Love is the only tool that will serve you in every situation. ♥ ♥ ♥

Change

This concluding chapter of the book in many ways is the joker in the pack – or the ace that changes the game. Some hate change; some embrace it. Some use it; others don't know how to handle or try to ignore it. But it will come. You will change; your mind will change. Technology will change. Your customers will change. The economy will change. This chapter helps you stay mindful, aware, alert, fluid, free and flexible.

Read this chapter when you or things around you, your business or the environment are at a point of transition or when you feel stuck or inspired to mix things up. ♥ ♥ ♥

CLARITY

Know who you are;
walk your unique path

If you're not clear then nothing will be...

Finding oneself and one's path is like waking up on a foggy day.
Be patient, and presently the fog will clear and that which has always
been there can be seen. The path is already there to follow.

Perhaps the most common theme that people come to me with as a coach is the want for clarity, focus and a sense of direction, personally, professionally and in business. Very often we feel as though we're not clear, we're not certain and we want a very clear path to where it is that we're going.

This chapter of the book will help you develop clarity about who you are, why you are in business and where you are going. It will also help you ensure that you continue to give yourself space and remain clear throughout your business journey. Let's begin:

- ♥ Who are you?
- ♥ Why are you here?
- ♥ Why are you in business?
- ♥ Why are you thinking of going into business?
- ♥ What is it that business means to you?
- ♥ What is it that you're wanting to achieve from your business?
- ♥ Are your goals and aspirations the same today as they were yesterday?

These are very, very important questions that we need to look at. Take a little time to ask yourself these questions, whether you've been in business for 20 years, have just finished studying or are thinking of giving up the career that you've been in. Each year I meet many established business owners who are unclear about the answers to these questions. Once you are clear – and happy with the answers – many of the doubts you have will lessen and may even vanish.

Your journey: the balancing act of business

Working as a coach to business owners, I've discovered that there are three aspects of running a fulfilling business:

1 **You:** Without you, your health, your motivation and your heart there is no business. It is an aspect of business many overlook. Your journey must start here. Starting here you will be clear, motivated and able to take care of yourself and what is most dear to you in life. Business is merely one aspect of life – you must not lose sight of that. If you do, you may perhaps build a 'successful' business but you will remain unfulfilled and may have paid too high a price.

2 **Your business:** What is the type or nature of your business? What rules and regulations will apply? What shape, structure, staffing, systems, policies and procedures will need to be in place? Without an effective management and operations approach or model, your business will struggle. These things may need to change over time, and there will be challenges involved.

3 **Your customers and market:** Who are your customers and potential customers? What do they want and how do they want it? How do they see the world? What is going on in your marketplace and with competitors? How can you best serve them? What do your customers want from you specifically? How will you stay in touch with and address changes that affect your customers and the wider environment?

FIGURE 1.1   The three aspects of business

It is the space in Figure 1.1 where *you, your business* and *your customers/your market* intersect that the exceptional soul trader business really resides. It's here that the focus must be developed and the success of your business will be shaped.

What's your story?

So who are you? What's your story? I'm amazed by the number of times that business owners don't ever stop to consider their unique story. Your story is important; it may well have led you here. It may well hold valuable clues to what you want and what you can contribute. Increasingly customers want to know who it is you are and why you're doing what it is that you're doing. **And very often you and your own unique story may be all that separate you from others in the market.** There will be thousands of other accountants, therapists, web designers, cake makers, solicitors and shop and restaurant owners; so what is it that makes you special?

Cast your mind back over your life and career story to date. What is it that actually brought you to this point of starting your business or growing it? Run through your life and career to date. Then take a moment simply to write it down, using Table 1.1, in a couple of sentences that encapsulate your story.

TABLE 1.1 My story

My story to date
Why I'm in business (or why I'm planning to start a business)

Now I want to invite you to go one step further forward. Gently think about what you want to do and contribute and how big it is that you dream. What do I mean by this? Well, it's very important for you to have an idea of what it is that *you* actually want from business. I've coached scores of people who have been frustrated (often for years or decades) by following someone else's dream of what they should be and what they should achieve. It may also be that you've been frustrated by your progress but have never asked yourself what *precisely* you want to achieve – and why.

How big do you dream? Some people like to climb mountains; others like to go for casual strolls in the hills. What is it that's really important to *you*? Do you want a chain of shops? Do you plan to produce a range of products that get sold in lots of stores? Or is it something simpler? For example, one of my clients intends always to remain the only employee in his business, but his goal is to attract more affluent customers on a higher fee, with a waiting list, and possibly to introduce a few products.

Along the journey the shape, size and indeed specifics of your dream may change. You might start out with big dreams and then think 'Actually, I want to scale that down – I want a simpler life and business.' The opposite can happen too. You may start off with small aspirations and then think 'I want to take on some staff, diversify, produce some products and open some stores.' Your dream is all within your gift, so I invite you to spend just a little bit of time with this. How big is it that you dream? What precisely is it that you want to create?

What might the journey involve?

Clarity is also about knowing what your journey to develop your business might involve. The metaphor of climbing a mountain on the one hand or a gentle hill on the other is an apt one. Many dream of climbing mountains, but few do. Some think climbing mountains is easier than it is. It may be unclear exactly how difficult it is until you try. It will take a combination of mental strength, vision, ability and the right team, training, research, strength, support, supplies and shelter. The risks can be huge, and not everyone makes it. Some are foolish, do not learn the lessons from others and are ill prepared. It may be possible to climb gentler slopes with less preparation, planning, resources, self-belief, support or insight. We can perhaps afford to make assumptions about climbing hills. What is it that *you* seek to gain: the experience, the prestige, the conquering achievement, the comradeship?

I remember working with a business owner who had run a café in the past. Her new business venture involved a very big dream, huge logistics and lots of unknowns and variables. She was caught up in her new dream and hadn't thought through what it would actually involve to turn it into reality. It was only when I stopped and asked her the reality of setting up a café – from the dream to the everyday reality – that she realized what was involved in her new venture. She talked through her journey of setting up the café, from finding premises right down to the day-to-day routines of ordering supplies, endless washing up, and getting customers through the doors to pay the rent! She realized that she had to become more realistic about her new business and work out – just as with her café – all the steps it would take to plan, start up and run.

I will never forget an occasion when I was running a Your Life, Your Business workshop. I'd prompted the attendees to consider where they were and their next steps. To help illustrate this, I had put up a slide of a person at the wheel of a boat. In the image you could see a little of the boat, a little of the seas and skies around and a hint of land in the distance. As everyone was quietly relating the image to their own journey, a woman suddenly exclaimed 'I have a hole in my boat!' She explained that there were logistics in her business that were flawed; the premises that she was planning to use needed work, and some of her systems needed developing. She had identified specifics that related to her that she needed to take care of and fix. Though she was new to her business and was still learning, this analogy helped her understand her business, its needs and the task ahead more clearly.

No metaphor or analogy – or indeed any endeavour you've under-taken before – will completely hold up or hold true to where you are now. But they can give insight, clarity and a quick virtual reality check on our ideas and the possible path ahead. This is true not only if you're starting out.

Anand has been in business all his adult life, but was lacking clarity on how to move forward. He is a keen golfer, so I asked him to relate where he was in his business and his challenges as if in a game of golf. He explained he had the wrong grip and too tight a grip in business, which in golf would be a disaster. Taking a metaphor he knew well and relating it to his business, where he was struggling with clarity, helped. He's making the adjustments and has a lighter, more effective 'touch' with his business clients and contacts. The golf metaphor helped him gain even more clarity by looking at the wider environment of his business and relating the competition to other players and challenges to bunkers. I'm often astounded, in working with business owners, at how profound such metaphors can be and how precisely we can identify valuable, useful learning and apply it.

Your vision and values

Once you are clear about what's really important to you in your life, your business and the people, it will help clear your mind, clear the way ahead and clear away the distractions. It is no surprise that we use the word 'visionary' of those who have innovated and pioneered. It comes from a clear-sightedness. It comes from knowing what is important and what is not. Until *you* are clear nothing will be. Until you know what is important you will not know what to focus on, where you are going, where you are heading or even what is going on. We live in a world where we are overwhelmed by data, distractions and things to do. Stopping and looking will help you become clear on who you are, what your drivers are, where you are going and what paths are worth taking. It will serve you in every personal and professional situation. It will help you cut through the noise and the nonsense and be true to yourself. Clarity and focus – followed by motivation – are the top issues with which people come to me as a coach. From clarity all else can happen and flow. You will not get very far in heavy fog. It will slow you down and can cause some serious damage to yourself and others. If you take a little time and space and look closely, the fog can clear and be replaced by a sharpness of vision that can propel you forward.

This is an exercise that I do with almost everybody I work with, because it's really important, before you start on this journey of building your business and building it by heart, that you know exactly what it is that you want to build. So we're about to find out exactly what's important to you in your life; we're going to find out exactly what's important to you in your business; and we're going to find out exactly what's important to you in terms of relationships with people. In this way, you'll be very clear of how you want your business to look, how you want your life to be, and what types of people and relationships you want in your life.

Use Table 1.2 and write down a list of 6 to 10 words of what's most important to you in life, 6 to 10 words of what's most important to you in business, and 6 to 10 words of what's most important to you in relationships. So, for example, not long ago I was working with a woman whose 'Life' list included the words *fun, family, health* and *well-being*. In her 'Business/career' list she wrote words that included *children, contribution* and *money*, because she was passionate about helping children and she recognized that generating money from her business was important and something she had overlooked in the past. In her 'Relationships' list she put words including *trust, fun* and *respect*.

But what's really important here is *your* words. We don't want anybody else's stuff. If you're not careful your entire career can be driven by other people's list of 'stuff'. This might be your first opportunity of asking yourself what it is that you want. This is absolutely imperative. We don't want Mum, Dad, Uncle Bob or some magazine's idea of what it is that you should have or should aspire to. It's your list. It may include specific things or intangible or even ethereal things that are very important to you. I invite you to let your heart write the list. Use the top half of the table; we'll be using the numbered section later.

TABLE 1.2 My values, or what's most important

LIFE	BUSINESS/CAREER	RELATIONSHIPS
1.	1.	1.
2.	2.	2.
3.	3.	3.
4.	4.	4.
5.	5.	5.
6.	6.	6.
7.	7.	7.
8.	8.	8.
9.	9.	9.
10.	10.	10.

Great, so you've got a whole list of words there. You might have words like *health, happiness, success, fun, making a difference, travel, security, technology* or whatever it might be. But it's important to know precisely what these words mean to *you*. Success might mean one thing to you and something completely different to your best friend or partner. Not being clear what your definition of success – or anything else – is can cause a lot of unnecessary confusion, in business especially, if it is never articulated and explored. So for some people success might mean a string of shops internationally and a yacht, while for you it might mean being your own boss and doing what you love working from home.

It's really important that you find out precisely what these words mean to you. What does each word mean? What would it be like? What would it look like if it were in place? If it helps, you may write a short definition of each word on a piece of paper. For example, for one client of mine *free time* meant Friday afternoon through to Sundays free for her and her family. This simple clarifying helped her to shape and manage her life and business.

Once you've meditated on each word and clarified what it means to you, use the second half of the table to put the words in each of the three lists in order of importance. Now this may be difficult, because we already know that everything in your lists is important, but the mere process of considering 'Actually, is health more important than love?' or 'Is well-being more important than fun?' may well bring certain things to the fore. It may bring a great deal of insight, clarity and simplification to your life.

Spend some time with your list. It will be valuable if you are thinking about starting a business, and it will also be valuable if you have been in business for some time. The purpose, as with writing a shopping list, is just to help us be absolutely clear about what it is we want and to help create focus.

I want to invite you to do one more thing. Consider what things are already in place. When you go shopping, if you're not careful, you can rush out before checking and using what you already have – and lo and behold you might end up with a fridge and a cupboard full of things that are out of date. So what things are already in place in your life, business and relationships? Sit with this and really be grateful. Give yourself credit for all the things that are already there in place in your life. I often work with people for whom many of the things that are really important are already in place.

Anthony is an IT expert, qualified pilot and budding inventor. He's employed but desperate to get his own business up and running, and his anxiety was becoming counter-productive. He has remarkable things in place: strong, rich family relationships. In fact most of the things in his 'Life' and 'Relationships' lists were in place. It was only when he stopped to notice and acknowledge this that he realized the powerful achievement he had already made in his life and relationships and the strong base this provided for moving forward. He was overly caught up with what wasn't in place, overlooking what he had, and this was having a knock-on effect on his way of approaching business. Now, instead of being agitated and approaching business from a perspective of 'lack', Anthony is more relaxed, patient and appreciative and works from his strengths. He is taking self-responsibility and focusing on what he does have and can do. He is now utilizing his personable qualities to attract the right people in to help him. And, instead of waiting for some ideal time, he is working on some of the business ideas that he can develop, including a cookery business idea that he has already made some headway in. So give yourself credit for all of the things that are already in place. It's extremely important.

Now the question is: 'Is your business based on the things that you're really passionate about or is it based on something else?' Casting your eye across those lists will give you some very valuable information, so I want you to meditate on them. What would your life look like if these things were in place? What would your business and your career look like if these things were in place? And what would your relationships look like if these things were in place?

Carmen runs a health and fitness website. She got in touch when she felt she had lost motivation and direction. When she put her 'Life' list in order of importance she realized that there was actually an order of events that needed to be in place to get her back on track. For her the first word was *health*; if health was in place then she would have *energy*, which was the next thing on her list. *Support* was next. She realized that, if she had energy, she could seek the support she wanted in life. *Fun* was next. She realized that, with health, energy and support, her life and business would then be fun – and she was a fun person. Overall this simple exercise gave her powerful clarity on how she wanted her life to be and, more importantly, how she needed to be and what needed to be prioritized to get the sense of direction and motivation back.

Shabi had put her own dreams on hold for many years whilst she was a carer for her parents and worked in the family business, so it was a challenge for her to get clarity on what *she* wanted. I got her to do the values exercise and simply invited her to meditate on her lists for the two weeks until we met next. She came back and she said 'Rasheed, this is precisely what I'm wanting to do.' Her chosen field was patient care, and despite her own health challenges she followed up with training and volunteering. She is now moving toward working part time in a field that she is passionate about: helping and being an advocate for others to live as active lives as they can with their health conditions. Her new path combined being an advocate for others – which she had always had an interest in – and patient health, which had emerged as a topic very dear to her heart.

The supermarket of life

There's something else that's very important in establishing clarity. It's wise to consider what kind of a character you are. If the values lists that you've completed related to going shopping, you'd find that there are three different types of shopper in life:

- ♥ **Shopper 1: the list shopper.** If you are this shopper, you always go out with a list of what you want. You won't leave home without that list of what you are going to buy from the supermarket or from the clothes stores and so on. *Advantages:* You are clear and focused. You save time and often money. You are not easily distracted. *Disadvantages:* You can be overly focused and may miss other opportunities. You may also not always find what you want – or it may not be where you're looking for it. You become overwhelmed if the list is too long.

- ♥ **Shopper 2: the 'no list' shopper.** If you are this shopper, you go out with no list at all. You're the kind of person who is at peace, in flow. You may already know what you want or you may be open to life's possibilities – or you may be unorganized or unconcerned. *Advantages:* You may spot opportunities and bargains, and you may enjoy the journey more than others and be less disappointed than them. *Disadvantages:* You may be overwhelmed and ineffective and spend too much time and money on things you don't need.

♥ **Shopper 3: the 'I don't want' shopper.** If you are this shopper, you have a list of the things that you don't want. Now you might say 'Rasheed, who on earth has a list of things that they don't want?' But stop and think about it. You probably know people who are always saying 'I don't want this' – 'I don't want this job', 'I don't want this relationship', 'I don't want this happening to me' – and, lo and behold, everything tends to pertain to the things that they don't want, and their heads are so full of the things that they don't want that they're not aware of the things that they do want. *Advantages:* None – other than it being a prompt to identify what you do want. *Disadvantages:* You will constantly find things that you don't want. You may feel confused, misunderstood and even a victim. You may lack self-responsibility.

Overall, when it comes to business and life, most people are a blend of these characters, but many of us have one dominant trait. If you are the third type of shopper you must quickly take the best intention from it and incorporate parts of shopper 1 or 2 that work for you. If you are one of the other types of shopper, what is it that works for you? Do you need to have a very clear list of what's really important to you, or do you work best actually with a little bit of a free rein? Do you like to shop alone or with others? Do you tend to research first? Would you rather have someone else do the actual shopping part for you?

So know what kind of a shopper you are. Know what kind of a business person you are in order that you can build your business 'in your own style and image'. It also means that you can quickly overcome hurdles and challenges. Perhaps you are a social shopper and like shopping with others, which may also explain why you feel isolated if you are in business alone or without any support. How can you involve others formally or informally? Or perhaps you're setting up and don't understand some of the procedures – in which case it might be best to get someone else to help you understand and sort out the process of setting up, registering and so on. You may need others to help you.

By applying the values list and 'supermarket of life' insights you can become far clearer and more focused and productive.

Your passion, mission and purpose

Let's get even more clarity and look at your passion and purpose. Interestingly, most successful and effective people in all walks of life tend to share three common characteristics:

- ♥ **vision:** a clear vision, cause, purpose or mission;

- ♥ **belief:** in themselves, their product, the cause, and others;

- ♥ **action:** focused, flexible, customer-orientated, planned, brave, considered and intuitive.

Whether you're intending to be a very successful serial entrepreneur or just to do your own thing, low-key, earning you a living, it's very important that you're absolutely in tune with what it is that you're about.

I'm going to invite you to write three sentences that will help to crystallize what you and your business are about:

- ♥ **'My passion is...'** This may well just be a long list of things. It might be that you're passionate about making a difference, sports cars, shoes, clothes, music, technology, creating things, whatever it might be. Write your list. It doesn't need to relate purely to business; it might be things you're passionate about in your world or in the world generally.

TABLE 1.3   My passion

My passion is...

♥ 'My mission is...' What is your goal or objective, personally or professionally? It may relate to business, or it may relate to your life and world more widely. My mission, for example, is to help people of all backgrounds to find greater fulfilment in all areas of their lives, careers and relationships from within. Ultimately my mission is about raising our consciousness.

Here are two missions of differing emphasis that fit the owners' style and drivers: 1) 'Establishing a business delivering fresh fruit to people's homes to boost health and fitness – starting out in New York and then expanding across the country and to Europe in the coming five years.' 2) 'Running a sports business that gives my family a good quality of life, and being the best father that I can possibly be.'

Write yours. Don't be influenced by others. Do not let your head edit yourself here. Let what wants to come through come through. It may well be very personal and very 'you' orientated, or it may relate to others. Most important is that it really rings true and that you're motivated by it. You may be very surprised. It may link to what you've always done or be something that has remained unsung by you. Incidentally, the 'mind' loves very specific missions, as it can quite quickly begin to assess and identify what the steps to achieve this might include.

TABLE 1.4   My mission

My mission is...

♥ **'My vision is...'** If you like, the vision is what the world or
your world would look like if you were to achieve your
mission. Let's imagine that your mission is to create
beautiful, hand-made children's shoes. Your vision might be
a world in which kids went to school with shoes that fitted
them and that they didn't develop foot problems. In the case
of my vision, given that my mission is to help people find
greater fulfilment in all areas of their lives, it would be a
world where people are more at peace with themselves and
each other and a raised consciousness. The vision for the
healthy fruit and vegetable delivery business might be
'Creating healthier, happier families'.

TABLE 1.5   My vision

My vision is...

Great, hopefully you've got some sentences written down. They might be very specific or a little bit fuzzy. That's fine. Live with your statements; leave them and come back to them. Fine-tune them. Take as long as you need. Visions and missions often develop over months and indeed throughout the life of a business. The clearer you are the more compelling you will be, but let your heart clarify this picture.

Once again: are you doing what it is that you're passionate about or are you doing something else? Very often, when I work with business owners of all types – including some successful business owners – what happens is that there's a real disconnect between what they're doing and what they want to be doing.

There are times along the journey where you may review or readjust your business around your values, or your values may change. Helen is a friend and contact who began her career in teaching and academia, retrained as a solicitor, and later made the shift to train as a massage therapist to get in touch with the holistic side of life. She then established a business helping therapists and other small businesses generally with their legal matters, which is when we met. Having done this for several years, and having had her fill of busy city life, Helen has a new and simple mission: enjoying her new life in the country, writing, and making delicious food for family, friends and neighbours. So it's the case that your mission may well develop or even change throughout life and in line with what sits with your priorities in life.

It may be that there is a gap between your values, vision and mission and what you're doing. Are you following somebody else's dream? Do you have the courage to build your business on what is most true to you? There may be a gap between what you're doing in your business and what's important in life. Sometimes it can be bridged if your business income enables you to do the things that are truest to you in your heart. If you are clear about that, then fine. If not, you may need to consider now what the business (or the business change) is that is most true to you.

In most cases, for the hundreds of people I have coached, there comes a point where all the different skills, talents they have and aspects of the jobs they have done that most resonate with them meet. You may feel that your life, career and business to date have been a random mix, but there will be a link if you look gently but deeply.

In my own case the seemingly strange mix of working in press and PR and then going off to become a singer and along the way volunteering as a Samaritan and then becoming a coach all seemed haphazard at one point, even though I had 'chosen' each path. It was when I added the last part of becoming a speaker that it all made sense. One day I had to speak at one of my first big exhibitions. I'd just recorded my second audio download, 'Become who you are'. My first one was very generic, but this second product was truer to me. I realized when I landed the speaking gig and had to decide on the topic that I had to follow my heart and deliver 'Become who you are'. The moment I walked out to the audience I remembered what it was to be a singer. There was a meeting place between all of these elements: the media, the singer, the speaker, the coach and the trainer. The common thread was the ability to connect to others and to enable those others to connect to themselves and their magic. Everything since (and indeed before) has been an offshoot and manifestation of that.

So, over the coming days and weeks, continue to meditate on what your life and your business would be like and look like if they were truest to your heart. This is not something to 'think' about. By all means put the question to your mind. Let your mind go off and go about its business, but the answer it comes back with must come from a deeper and truer place. It must ring true with your heart. This is the same whether you've been in business for 15 years and feel stuck or whether you are starting out.

From strengths to threats – looking ahead

It is not enough to be clear about what you're passionate about and where you want to go. You need to be clear about your strengths and playing to them. It is this that is the mark of a champion.

I've worked with countless business owners where, for example, in their promotional literature and on their websites they failed to list major clients and career accomplishments and plaudits, when the only difference between them and their competitors was that their competitors had promoted and made use of their achievements. Are you playing to your strengths?

In Table 1.6 list all your skills, talents and accomplishments and all you've overcome. List the personal talents and skills and the professional ones. The same words may appear in both lists. This may bring you more clarity and confidence. Very often over the course of a life and career, confidence can be knocked down rather than developed. If that's been the case for you then this is especially important. You may also find that there are some nuggets that may be useful in terms of things you may have overlooked, areas that you might specialize in, things you could use to promote yourself

TABLE 1.6   Strengths, skills, talents, accomplishments, qualifications, and challenges overcome

Personal	Professional

and your business – or simply skills you could further exploit. Take time with this exercise. Be exhaustive in all you've achieved in your life and career – this goes far beyond a career résumé or CV. Some of your most subtle skills, talents or achievements may be the most profound. But likewise if you've served major clients, brought in large amounts of business for a previous company or been part of an award-winning team then these specifics must be captured so that you can truly utilize them.

I was recently working with Ash, a computer expert who had the idea of developing a comparison-style website business. I got him to complete the skills exercise that you've just completed and the strengths, weaknesses, opportunities and threats (SWOT) exercise that follows. The combination helped him to develop his original idea and to fast-track his transition into business by using his real strengths and starting up his business as an IT consultant.

So let's get even more clear about the path ahead by completing the strengths, weaknesses, opportunities and threats analysis. It is a simple tool but a powerful one, which is why many businesses of all sizes use it in strategic planning. It can very quickly identify key issues to be addressed, developed and exploited.

Karen has run a boutique recruitment business for two years and has a couple of major clients. She is now keen to take her business the next step forward and bring in some new clients, which will enhance her business, finances and quality of family life and help fund more quality time away. Completing the SWOT exercise in detail gave us *opportunities*: a specific long list of contacts to focus on as leads to pursue for potential work. Her *strengths* majored around her excellent people skills and subject knowledge and personable, customer-focused style. This gave us the strategy that we needed; she is great with people, but just wasn't having enough conversations to bring in the two or three new clients she seeks. I gave her some tips that we will look at in Chapter 5 ('Conversations'). Likewise we identified some *threats* in her field of recruitment to keep an eye on. The great news was that she could advise her clients on these threats, which are industry issues, so she could turn aspects of this threat into an opportunity. We also identified *weaknesses*. The main one was limited resources and staff. This is common in almost all sole trader and micro businesses. Her business is largely herself and a few associates, and this highlighted some steps she could take to broaden her pool of associates. It also raised the question of her long-term ambitions and whether she might perhaps want to branch out and set some more ambitious goals.

Take some time with the SWOT that follows. It is important that you are thorough and specific. The sample SWOT may be useful. The more specific you can be with the who, what, why, how much and how many, the more value you will get from it and the easier it will be actually to develop your business. You may want to complete it or leave it and come back to it. Ask yourself 'What's missing?' and add anything else that comes to mind. Then imagine that you are a professional outsider looking in – perhaps someone who is privy to knowing about your background and your relevant business environment. In fact you may wish to go that one step further and work on your SWOT with a skilled expert in your field whom you know, like and trust. The person may be a colleague, a business partner or someone who runs a business. It may be someone in your (planned) field.

Strengths and weaknesses relate to you and your business, team, skills and resources specifically. They will tend to relate largely to internal factors. Opportunities and threats, which are largely external factors, tend to include opportunities around and related to you and threats to you and your business, many of which relate to others in the market or are broader social, political and environmental factors.

Table 1.7 shows an example of Judy's PR business. Judy has worked in PR for years and set up on her own last year. You'll notice that the weaknesses and threats have prompted Judy to identify some things she needs to act on. The SWOT could be further developed by fleshing out further opportunities and contacts to approach, and there may be other threats and weaknesses that she has not yet thought of.

TABLE 1.7   Judy's PR business SWOT

Strengths:	Weaknesses:
Qualified journalist. Ten years' experience working with major agencies, including XYZ. Contacts in national and local TV, radio and press. Strong written, verbal and general people skills. A passion for PR and media. Won PR team of the year award at XYZ. Can work from home, with low overheads.	No business experience. Little finance experience (need better skills). Limited start-up cash; no savings. Working from home (need space for meetings). Old computer (need 123 model and software, and back-up in case of crashes). Have only two clients (need six per month). Shy at promoting self (time to change).
Opportunities:	Threats:
Doing PR event for previous employer. Team up with Bill, who's thinking of leaving work. Working with Margaret, who runs internet marketing company to refer business. Attend trade shows to develop contacts. Approach new firm that's just moved into the area to do a story on them and approach to do their PR. Join some PR and media forums online. Upgrade website and have some free tools that could be promoted. Ask previous clients for referrals and ask Bob for introduction to DEF Ltd. Running PR workshops for small business organizations (need to research or join some too). Overcome nerves and give more general talks and workshops to attract business. Build links with web developers, admin assistants and professional services so that we can refer business. Promote client stories in quiet summer months.	Fire, theft, flood. Internet or computer crash or problems. Other PR consultants and small businesses. Larger (or small firms) trying to steal clients! Logistics/supplier problems at shows or events. Tough climate for events companies. Online PR services, or people doing their own. Illness or injury to myself. Adverse publicity affecting clients or self. Summer months are quiet in PR terms (need to address this: save cash or find opportunity).

TABLE 1.8 My SWOT

Strengths:	Weaknesses:
Opportunities:	Threats:

Judy might also choose to put down a price next to her new computer and the type of software she needs. She has also not listed a weakness she has about not being on some key press databases and mailing lists that would be advantageous to her.

As you turn to your own SWOT in Table 1.8, be as detailed and specific as you can, and where you identify weaknesses note what actions you need to take. This might include skills to develop or simply research that you need to do or things to find out about.

Hopefully you've got a sense of where it is you're going, the issues to address and some avenues you could take. Let's take this further. Most large organizations and many businesses have three- or five-year plans. On the one hand, this is purely wishful thinking; none of us can predict what's going to happen in five years' time. On the other hand it's very important, because it gives you (and your team) clarity and focus about where you want to be.

Where is it that you would like to be in your life and your business:

- ♥ in 10 years' time?
- ♥ in three years' time?
- ♥ in one year's time?

Spend at least 10 minutes mulling it over, write down what comes through and see how it sits with you. Are you motivated by it? Does it feel true to your heart, or is it just ego?

These three differing timeframes can be useful. Often the 10 years' time picture may relate to lifestyle factors: you want to be retired, to have reached a certain stage in business or to be spending more time with the people you love or on travel or pastimes. Three years and one year tend to bring into focus clarity on specific goals.

Give some thought to the three pillars of your business:

- ♥ **Finance:** What do you want or need to make? What systems and support need to be in place?
- ♥ **Marketing:** Where do you fit and how do you want to be found, seen and perceived?
- ♥ **Operations:** What shapes, size, structure and level of staffing do you want?

Of course, what you find on the journey may be radically different, and the technology and the world that we find ourselves in may be very different. But at least you've got a sense of where it is you're wanting to be, and that's extremely important for any journey.

This clarity will help you to forge ahead with building your business from your heart. It may also bring up other questions or thoughts such as 'Hang on a minute, you know what, I've got to this point in my business and I don't think this business is for me' or 'I don't think business is for me any more.' But hopefully what you've uncovered so far will have given you the clarity to start, to make changes, to build or to reshape your business.

This is exactly where Steve is. Steve is a talented graphic designer who has worked in a range of sectors and has run his own T-shirt business in the past. He has had a few setbacks and family matters to address, and has been out of the loop for a few years. He's now ready to build his career again and is clear about his love for design. He now needs to clarify what kind of work he wishes to do, whether he wishes to work alone or with others and how much money he needs to make. He has some leads and opportunities. In some ways he's been there and done it, and in some ways he's starting out. The exercises and questions covered in this chapter have helped him ask himself deep questions. What is clear is that he wants to make a living from what he loves and that he wants rich, positive relationships in life and with those he works with, based on his values and his talent.

If you are ready you may wish to turn your attention to the two-page business plan tool in Chapter 6 ('Creativity'). Turn to it whenever it feels right. It may be you wish to begin to complete it now, filling in the section about your vision and goals, and you can continue to work on it as you make your way through the chapters. Alternatively you may wish to wait until you have completed the book in its entirety.

Staying clear

You've already covered a lot of ground; you are clearer about your story, your values, your mission, your goals and your strengths. But there is another aspect of clarity that is extremely important. You will need to remain clear throughout the journey. You will need to continue to check in, monitor your progress, step back, gain perspective and focus.

Be it that you're thinking of starting out or looking to grow, you are going to need space. You will need space because like windows we gather dust, so we will always need to stop to get clear again. Things will shift for you, in your life and in your business. Your values and priorities may well change, and giving yourself space is key.

To keep clear you will need: regular time and space to review your goals and progress; and physical space to see clearly and arrange what you need to do. We will expand on these themes in Chapter 6 ('Creativity').

Space if you are starting out

You might need to book some time off work in order to plan, research, read up about business, find out what's involved, talk to people who have run their business before, and find out all sorts of information. You'll need or should give yourself time to talk to people you know and love, those who have *been there and done it*. You'll need to give yourself space and a chance to dip your toe in the water and to feel comfortable about business – perhaps to plan out your finances and to set a survival budget of what you'll need to bring in. You'll also need to give yourself the time actually to develop your business over the coming months. By doing so you will develop greater clarity.

Space if you are in business

When it comes to clarity there is a close relationship between space and time. It's incredibly important that you build in time, as you are doing now, to review your business, because there are two businesses you're running at once. There is the actual business – all the practical stuff of operating your business – and then there is the 'business' of actually moving that business forward. It's what is classically called the difference between working 'in' the business and working 'on' the business.

- ♥ How much time do you spend running your business and how much on developing it?
- ♥ How much time do you need to take out away from your business?
- ♥ Do you have an adequate work–life balance?

Do you need to readdress that balance? I read a beautiful interview with the actor Jim Carrey recently. He was talking about success and what he's learnt throughout his life, and he said that, if somebody builds a successful business but they are estranged from their family, then they've failed. If you've got things in your life list that are very, very important around things like family then it is important that you do not see your business as being divorced from that or you may end up divorced.

This is the opportunity to ask yourself: 'What precisely would a good work–life balance be like for me?' 'How much time and how much space do I need to build in?'

Stepping back to review your business

One of the things I do as a coach is to get clients to build in those times. It is the most common problem for businesses. Business owners lack clarity and focus because they do not step back often and strategically enough. Put in a 10-minute weekly review where you can pause, step back and review your business. I suggest 10 minutes because I know it's achievable. Chapter 6 ('Creativity') will help you to develop the right framework to plan, perform at your best and rest. It will also prompt you to ensure you put in free time, family time and creative time. Time away from the business and rest are a key part of clarity. Without them you will be unable to focus or be productive.

Keeping it simple

The simpler you make things the clearer they will be. Think a little bit about what the systems are that you need to put in place. If you've been in business for some time you might already be aware that there are some things that need to be simplified or systematized. What things need to be taken care of?

- ♥ What needs to be strategized?
- ♥ What needs to be simplified?
- ♥ What things need to be systematized?
- ♥ What things do you need to stop doing?
- ♥ What things do you need to start doing?

Make space: 'You cannot pour more water into a full cup'

If your mind, life or business is cluttered you will not have the clarity you need to excel in business. Very often when I'm coaching people what I get them to do is throw things out. Have a clear-out at your home and your office. Recycle, pass on or give away what you can and throw out what you cannot. There's a relationship between a cluttered office and home and a cluttered mind. The act of throwing out old files and making space can be powerful. Just because things are out of sight in cupboards and files does not mean that they are out of mind. The process of clearing out your office, shop, desk, room or home will lighten your mind and make you feel lighter and sharper. Do not wait until spring to spring-clean. We live in a world of 'stuff': stuff in our minds and stuff in our lives. We live in a world of over-stimulation. It is your job to manage the stimuli. I invite you to meditate on what space, systems and content actually work for you.

It's really important to give yourself space. For some reason we equate space and doing nothing with being passive. Taking time out is one of the most energizing things you can do. Business can have a huge amount of content, but without the space the content is going to be very, very claustrophobic for you in your business. We will return to this when we look at being creative to grow and stay centred.

Getting ready

So where are you now? What things are you going to need to address? Perhaps you need to do some planning. Perhaps you're going to need to get some equipment. Perhaps you're going to need to sort out a new telephone line. Perhaps you're going to need to get some stationery made. Perhaps you're going to need to work out a space that you can use within your home or to research office space or stall space or other suchlike. Perhaps you need to have a meeting with your business partners and investors to plan the next phase of your business. What are the areas where you need help or where you have blind spots? What are the skills you need to develop? The following short review will help you.

FIGURE 1.2   What I need to address

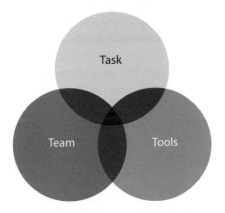

Taking stock: three-minute business review

1 What's already working well for a) you; b) your business?

2 How could you utilize these things more?

3 What's not working, and what are the problem areas or challenges you face?

4 What are the one to three things that should be prioritized that would have the best impact?

5 Identify the tools, resources and support you need.

6 Identify one thing to start doing and one thing to stop doing?

7 Identify one action that you will take as a result of this, and when will you do it?

What do you have and what do you need now?

You're probably now much clearer on where you are. The following simple exercise will help you to organize your next steps. List everything that you have and everything that you additionally need. Be very specific and comprehensive: include skills, experience, contacts, resources and money – everything that you have and may need. The more specific the better; for example, if you need to raise finance put in exactly how.

Chris is a wonderful lady I know who's long had a flair for unique antique-style clothes and hand-made jewellery. Table 1.9 shows what her list might look like. Use Table 1.10 for your own list.

TABLE 1.9   What Chris has and what she needs

I have...	I need...
10 years' experience in graphic design. Clothes- and jewellery-making experience. Experience running an office. Subscriptions to textiles magazines. A qualification in toy making. Storage space. A home office space. Two or three contacts in the fashion business.	An accountant. A website that can take payment. A web designer. To write a business and marketing plan. Some marketing skills and support. To sell an average of 20 items per month. A part-time admin assistant by next year. Approximately £15,000 to pay the admin assistant. A new computer for design next year (2k). Clearer systems for stock and mail-out. (I'd like) Someone to work with. To find and research local shows, fairs and distributors.

TABLE 1.10   What I have and what I need

I have...	I need...

SUMMARY

1 **What's your story:** Retrace it and embrace it. Now consider how you can utilize it.

2 **Know what's important:** Know your values and what's important in life, business and relationships. Stick to them and let them support and guide you.

3 **Your magic and passion:** Identify your skills, strengths and talents to let them clarify your business path.

4 **Your vision and mission:** Set the course that your heart desires – nobody else can.

5 **Get ready:** Identify the task and the tools, resources and support you'll need.

6 **Keep it simple:** Create space and simple systems. Act on what's important, and let go of what's not.

7 **Stay clear:** Make time to review progress, recharge your energy and reset your priorities.

Meditate on this chapter and what it is that your life and business need to look like in order to be true to your heart. How can you operate from this space from today? As much as we have touched on the future and goals, the future is born today. Yesterday is dead, and tomorrow may never arrive. The magic is here and now.

As my best friend once said to me as I talked about my goals, 'Make it where you are coming from, not where you are going to.' This changes the game. It means that all your aspirations and values, the journey and the work become internalized. Your sense of self or accomplishment is not dependent on it. No, it is who you are and what you are about.

We are now ready to connect with your customers...

CUSTOMERS

Build a business they will love

*Until you understand your customers – deeply
and genuinely – you cannot truly serve them.*

So what?

Whatever you're trying to sell me, I ain't buying it.

So you're clear why you're here, why you're running your business,
and what's really important to you in the rest of your life. You've
spent a little bit of time looking at your dreams, your goals and

your aspirations. Now we need to look at things from a completely different perspective. Ironically it's a perspective that many budding entrepreneurs and business owners completely forget about.

As you start or grow your business you can get so caught up in your dreams, your amazing product or your great idea that you can lose sight of one very important thing: your customer. Your customer is thinking: 'So what?' Your customer doesn't necessarily care about you, your dreams, your goals, your big product, your service or your aspirations. Your customer may well feel very nonchalant about you, your product and even your industry – or may be totally unaware of you.

So given everything that we've already covered, so what? So what of your dreams, your aspirations, your goals and your life story? It's really important that you arrive at this point of real humility to look again and look afresh.

One of the patterns that we've seen in recent times is big businesses especially that lose sight of their customers. Many lose touch with their customers and stop communication with them. When you choose to leave your phone company, utility supplier, bank, cable or satellite TV company – or any other – it's usually because you feel they have stopped listening, caring, or serving you properly, or are more focused on other customers. As with all relationships that wither, the interest and flattery they showed when you were court-ing has been replaced with complacency or non-communication. For a while, some big businesses can afford to lose old customers by attracting new ones. But you and your reputation may not be in that position. Successful soul trader businesses spring from winning customers over, keeping them enchanted and them auto-matically recommending you to their friends, family, colleagues and connections.

This is one of the reasons this book has two key chapters around customers. This chapter looks at your customers themselves. What is it that you actually know about them? What's going on in their world? Do they actually want your service or any other? What will make them buy? How do they want a product or service to look, feel and be promoted? And there are other such questions. The other chapter, 'Conversations' (Chapter 5), builds on this and will help you develop the dialogue that will win you business.

While writing this book I was called by Andy, a contact, who inspired by an earlier book of mine had decided to start up a live music night with a friend. He knew I had a singing background, and while both of them loved music neither had a business or entertainment background. They had identified a specific client base and were seeking a venue. As I listened to his idea I told him that now they were both clear on the dream they had to look at, research and address the needs of their three customer types: the audience/ venue attendees, the band or singers providing the entertainment and the venue owners. Having been a singer, performer and audience member at such nights and having known venue managers, I gave him an inside perspective of what he and his friend would need to consider to make it a success, including staging, lighting, having a live band rather than a backing track, fees for the band, and ideas to engage the audience to make it 'their night' that they'd bring friends to – the door numbers to keep the venue happy. I also urged him to talk to potential audience members and performers directly to get a wider perspective. Had they rushed ahead, as they initially wanted to, their dream might have ended abruptly, as they would have struggled to meet the band's and venue's needs and to get the balance, specifics and logistics right.

A friend told me of a yoga instructor he knew who produced beautiful, hand-made, soft fabric shoes for yoga. This instructor felt that the shoes would appeal, as people might want light, comfortable footwear to protect their feet gently instead of being barefoot. The instructor pushed ahead with producing hundreds of pairs, which hadn't sold and with which she was stuck, with a knock-on damaging effect on her finances. Had she asked people if they wanted such shoes and if so what shape, size, colour, texture and price? Had she thought about how they would be sold – directly or via fitness distributors? If the latter, had she developed relationships and contacts with the distributors? Had she asked them if there was a demand or if they would be interested in buying the shoes? I fear that she had not. Ironically my friend, who was developing his own product, was at risk of making some similar mistakes.

I call this the 'blindness of the visionary'. You can become so excited and so self-righteous that you lose sight of your customers (and your 'customers' may include suppliers, distributors and others). Sometimes this is complete blindness: you have the idea, do absolutely no research and throw your or others' money into it only to find that nobody wants it or that someone else is doing it better. Or you may be partially sighted: you look from the perspective of perhaps one or two client types and therefore miss lots of the information that you will actually need to produce, market and sell your product or service.

What's your situation? If you have dependants, a family, high living costs or other financial commitments and/or a product with premises, transport or stock costs, you need to ensure that you are thorough with your market research and customer research. I cannot stress this enough: if this is the case you have to conduct thorough customer research to support the exercises in this book or you may end up in major trouble. The exercises here will help you make a strong start, and the tips throughout the book will prompt you.

David is establishing a car parts business, which will involve all of these factors and considerable investment, costs and logistics. He is engaging with his industry contacts – his potential customers – and spending days on end at the British Library's Business and IP Centre to get his research right.

There is an additional factor to consider to ensure you get it right with your customers. There has been a shift in the balance of power in buying and selling. A generation or two ago people were reasonably open to advertising. It was still fairly new, and there were fewer outlets for it. Now adverts are not just on TV, radio, papers, magazines and billboards but everywhere: online, at ticket barriers at train stations, even on stairways. We are now hyper-attuned to it and how to block it out. People don't really want to be advertised to; when they want something they'll look for it. They don't want to be sold to. They don't want someone shoving a leaflet at them in the street or through their post box. They do not want a pop-up appearing on their computer screen whilst networking or watching a show online.

So you have a dilemma. As a business owner you want to get the message out there. But then there are your potential customers, who don't care – they want to be left alone.

The reality is that people are sick and tired of businesses selling to them when they often do not even know anything about the businesses or what their track record is. People are fed up of businesses that do not care about them and simply care about their cash. What's also true is that people see right through this selling approach, which is all about the businesses and has next to nothing to do with the customers.

This means that we need a whole new approach to marketing and sales based on genuinely developing a conversation and relationship. Later we will look closely at the kind of dialogue that may create rich possibilities for all concerned, but first of all we need to understand our customers deeply, so that we are able to engage with and serve them properly.

Customer scenarios

So I'm going to invite you to take off the hat of being who you are and running the business that you're running or planning, and I want you to look at life through the lens of your customer:

- ♥ Who are your customers?
- ♥ What do they want?
- ♥ What's really important to them?
- ♥ What are their concerns and their aspirations?

First let's map out who your customers are and what their needs, pain and problems are. It will give you insight into your differing

FIGURE 2.1 Mapping out your customers

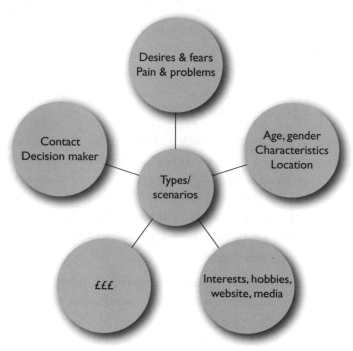

types of customer so that you can most effectively understand, identify with and engage with them. The first time I did this it was a revelation. Whether you're established and have done this before or are just starting out, this will give you insight into what your customers want and how to begin to engage with them.

Take a look at Figure 2.1. Now take a large piece of paper and let's map out your customers. It will help you to identify the different types of customers and, in the case of each different type of customer, to consider:

- ♥ their age and gender;
- ♥ their location;
- ♥ their pain and problems;
- ♥ their hobbies and interests;
- ♥ websites, media and social media they use;

♥ your competitors in this market;

♥ a rating from 0 to 10 on how lucrative this customer type is.

The secret is first to identify each different *type* of customer. I like to use the term customer 'scenario'. In other words, what is the situation or scenario that is going on for each potential customer? Thinking about the scenario will help you get to the heart of the situation and the psychology of your customer. We will expand on this in Chapters 4 ('Cooperation') and 5 ('Conversations'). Taking the time to get this right can save you huge sums of money in marketing and if acted on will help you gain business.

So my scenarios or types might include:

♥ someone who has just been made redundant or is facing redundancy;

♥ a business owner who is 'stuck';

♥ a business owner looking to grow the business;

♥ a person wanting to make a career change or find a new job;

♥ someone feeling lost or looking to find some direction;

♥ a person on a spiritual journey;

♥ someone in a high-profile job or in the public eye;

♥ a manager needing to motivate staff following a restructuring.

You may be reading this thinking 'In my case there are not differing scenarios; it's always the same.' That may be true for you but not your customer. Whether you make cakes or sell pensions, different customers have differing situations, mindsets, interests, tastes and preferences.

So the secret is to start with the large 'Type/scenario' branch and then draw lines branching out from there for each of your different scenarios or types of customer. It's not uncommon to have lots and need lots of space. Give each of these sub-branches a relevant name, as I have above.

From here you go around your piece of paper, branch by branch, and identify and write down the relevant information for each of the scenario types. So using my example I'd then look at my first subgroup, 'someone who has just been made redundant or is facing redundancy', and I'd ask myself what the age and gender are. I might put down 50/50 male and female, typical ages 35–55. Then I'd move on to the location and so on. You'll probably find that you know a lot about some customer types and scenarios and very little about others, and you may draw a blank on some parts and think 'I don't know where x type might be located' or 'I don't know who my competitors are in y.' This may be useful and point you to research that you need to do or it may help you to home in on the types of customers you know best.

Take your time and be as specific as you can be. Time and focus you spend on this now will have a direct relation to the time, energy and money that you may save yourself.

This exercise does not replace doing specific research as appropriate, but it may well set it off to a flying start and provide a clear focus for it. Depending on what stage of business you are at, you may wish to map out all the types or scenarios or focus on one or two. You may wish to draw a separate diagram for each type and scenario rather than having all the data from the different customer types on one crowded sheet.

In detail, the exercise is as follows:

- ♥ **Type/scenario:** Identify the type of customer or the scenario. Let's say you run a flower stall. Your types/scenarios might include: decorations for the home; a partner or loved one's birthday; forgetting a partner or loved one's birthday; a romantic dinner; flowers for a local restaurant; flowers for the reception of a local business; weddings; funerals; and so on. Draw a separate branch from the type/scenario heading and write the name of each type/scenario along that branch. Spend some time thinking about all the scenarios in which your product or service may be of use.

- ♥ **Age/gender:** Now consider the typical age (range) and gender breakdown for each type of customer. Let's use the example of the flower seller, who has perhaps identified that the first group, 'decorations for the home', is 80 per cent women and 20 per cent men and that the typical age range is 40–65 years old in both cases. Do the same for all the other client types/scenarios.

♥ **Location:** Where is each client group located? In some cases you may yourself choose to specify an area. Our florist may identify that the focus should be on only a three-mile radius for flowers for decorations and restaurants, but may identify the entire city for flowers for weddings and funerals, as the florist runs a website and can charge more for the occasion, justifying the transportation costs. If you run an online apps business, for example, it may well be that you identify a whole range of local and international markets where what you add may be appropriate for that language or culture. Location needs consideration – there may be all sorts of logistical issues for you and your customer.

♥ **Hobbies, interests, media and websites:** You need to get a clear sense of how to reach your customers and what they do. Understanding what publications, websites and media customers read or visit and what their hobbies are is invaluable. Let's imagine one of the customer types or scenarios for our florist is dating teenagers aged 14–16 at the local college. He might identify Facebook as one interest and medium. One of my clients provides management consultancy to senior managers. When we did this exercise he realized that many of his clients read *Management Today* and play golf. He may be wiser to target that title and to invest in a set of golf clubs rather than a scatter-gun marketing approach.

♥ **Competitors:** Who are your specific competitors for each client group? Do you know? Can you find out? Our flower stall seller may have identified that the competition for some services includes the two local supermarkets and the garden centre a mile away and, for other services like weddings or funerals, large online flower companies such as Interflora.

What's the case in your business? Is the competition for one type of client too fierce? Are you too inexperienced in one field for the moment? Is there a client group that you are overlooking where there is room for competition and where you are most skilled? All this information will be valuable as you begin to explore how you will reach your customer.

♥ **Pain/problems:** Marketing gurus drum on about this – and for good reason. We buy through desire and necessity. The fear, necessity and pain driver is generally stronger than the desire driver – but they are often related. Desiring flowers for the dinner table may not be as powerful a driver as needing flowers to dress the table to impress the boss you've invited for dinner. The pain and consequence of forgetting your wedding anniversary will be a more powerful driver to buy flowers than perhaps the thought of buying your spouse some on impulse. What's the pain and problem that your customers have in each scenario? It took me a long time to realize this in my business. I was targeting those who might want coaching rather than those who really needed it. The reality is that 90 per cent of people come to me because of a pain or problem in their life, career or relationships or with their team.

♥ **Contact and decision maker:** Who is the contact point and who is the decision maker involved? Let's say that a local business is one of the customers identified by our florist. The personal assistant to the managing director is the contact, and the managing director may be the decision maker. Similarly in your business, for each customer scenario, there may be two or three people or 'customers' involved, and your pitch and conversation to each may be very different. For the personal assistant, it may be about the prettiest flowers, while the managing director may care about value for money and standing out from competitors. This is one of the reasons we will spend a chapter on 'Conversations' (Chapter 5).

♥ **Money value:** Give a score from 1 to 10 for how valuable or lucrative each customer type or scenario is, with 1 being the lowest and 10 being the highest. Our flower stall seller may score his teenage audience only 2 out of 10, as they generally buy the least expensive flowers and buy infrequently. He may score the business 8, as they buy several large bunches of more expensive flowers and buy weekly. You may want to add an additional score so that you can give each type/scenario a 'one-off' and 'lifetime value' score. For example, the flower seller may score a wedding 10/10 for 'one-off', as the flowers are likely to be numerous and expensive, but a wedding may score only 1 in terms of lifetime value, as most people get married only once (or twice). The score could be different if the florist were based in Hollywood! This value score may be very useful for you. In one of my workshops, there was a business owner who'd set up a service for students, and she built a more successful business on this point alone. She had envisioned students would pay. This exercise and my prompting led her to explore a new business model by which she might focus on raising grants and funding so that the service was provided free or at a subsidized rate for students.

♥ What have you learnt?

♥ What do you know about your customers?

♥ What are the gaps in your knowledge?

♥ Where are the areas that you are most skilled at meeting customers' needs?

♥ Where do you face the most competition?

♥ What are the competition doing that you are not?

♥ Where do you have the edge?

♥ Do you need to carry out some more research on your customers, market, pricing or other areas?

♥ Do you need to narrow your focus? Do you need some additional skills or support? If so, what type? What should your priorities be?

There will always be questions in your business, and your ability to face them and answer them will be key to your success and progress.

Homing in on your place in the market

Waleed is a young entrepreneur who runs his own training and development business. Born in Saudi Arabia and well travelled, he holds a formal business qualification. He'd set up his business, website and marketing materials and was networking extensively, but he wasn't gaining the customers – and has a young family to feed. When he completed this exercise, we realized that he had a lot of competitors and he was younger and less experienced than most, so we focused on just two of his four target types. One was banking and financial services, where we identified a lot of 'pain and problems'. The second was manufacturing, where Waleed's engineering expertise around improving systems and processes was spot on to help address their pains. Suddenly from an approach where Waleed was a new entrant in personal development trying to be heard in the crowd, we had identified an area where his expertise, knowledge and service could help him stand out.

Seeing life through your customers' eyes

We tend to see business through our own eyes, but how is it your customers would want your business to look? How is it that they might want to experience your product or your service – from start to finish?

Today one of the key ways that potential customers see our stall is through our website. At some point, be it by doing a generic search for a product or service, by referral or through having met you, potential customers will look at your website. It is one of the key parts of your marketing portfolio and often one of the most costly. It is also something that many entrepreneurs labour over, as it brings into focus everything you do and what you are trying to convey.

Let's have some fun. Spend a few minutes thinking, as your customer, 'How would *I* want the website to look, feel and be set out?

What information would I want and how much?' Now spend 10 minutes sketching out how your client or your different types of clients would want your website to look, mindful of their pain, problems, needs and aspirations.

If you're already running a business, ask your customers how they would like the website to look. If you're thinking about starting your business, ask people whom you trust how they would like the website to look. Likewise, ask those who are your potential customers how they'd like the website to be.

As a coach, I look at hundreds of websites every year, and I'm amazed how many websites are similarly dull and uninspiring. 'We're blah, blah, blah and such a business' or 'We've been in business for over x years and we provide this, this and this to a very high quality.' Well, if everybody's business has that particular standard, how is it you're going to stand out? What is it that makes your business unique, and how would your customer want that information to be presented?

Thierry is a yoga teacher friend of mine who is developing a fitness product. He has been busy working on prototypes, engaging experts from designers to intellectual property lawyers, and running trial classes with his product to get feedback. He is on his third prototype. Each time he is getting more feedback, which is helping him fine-tune his product. The customer feedback has also identified new possible markets – especially footballers – he hadn't originally envisaged.

This process of looking at the business through our customers' eyes is exactly the one that Ben adopted. Ben used to work for a large firm of accountants, working long hours and lining other people's pockets, before deciding to branch out on his own. He realized that lots of people saw accountants as dull and distant. By networking and meeting such business owners he realized that they wanted a friendly accountant 'holding their hand' through the process of managing their finances. He also realized that they needed some simple tools to manage their finances. He then built his business, Accelerate Accounting, around this personable approach, helpful tools and consultancy, and it has really taken off, as the name he selected suggests.

In Chapter 5 we will look at the conversations you need to have with your customers to win their business, but first we need to check that you have the key 'tick boxes ticked' so that you're ready to approach customers:

- ♥ Do you actually have a business or just an idea at this stage?
- ♥ Do you actually have any content on your website?
- ♥ Have you tested the product that you want people to buy?

This is not just a question if you are starting out. After meeting an impressive entrepreneur who had won an award for helping dis- advantaged young people I searched for her website online to find out more to recommend her to others. But when I searched online I found very little information: just an unimaginative one-page website with little text, no pictures, no testimonials and no videos. If I had not met her first and I had just visited her website I would have taken it no further. Is this a situation that you are in? If you were a potential customer of your business and you searched for you or your business online, what would you find? Do it right now if you don't do it regularly. Would what you find impress you as your potential customer? I see this all the time: amazing people who either have no product or who are not communicating their product effectively. We will address much of this later in the book, but the question for you right now is this: 'Is your actual business or service up to scratch?'

Table 2.1 is an exercise to help you to understand your customers' thought processes and priorities.

First you need to identify your customers. You've already discovered some in the customer scenarios. You may want to pick a customer whom you need to get a greater insight into, a tricky type or a lucrative one. Now 'put yourself into their shoes': imagine you are the customer. Give yourself a moment to go into that character.

TABLE 2.1   Getting close to your customer

1.	What's your name (and post/title)?
2.	What's your scenario like right now personally/professionally?
3.	What's your pain and problem(s)?
4.	Would you like any help? If so what type?
5.	Where, when and how often do you want that help?
6.	What would you look for in the provider of this product or service?
7.	What's the a) most, b) least, and c) ideal price you'd like to pay?
8.	What would really make you buy?
9.	What might make you select a provider (or swap provider)?
10.	What might stop you buying this product/service?
11.	How would you like it packaged/presented/promoted?
12.	When and by what means would you like to be approached?
13.	Who is it best to approach and who makes the buying decision?
14.	How would you like to be kept in touch and served by a provider long-term?

You can either do this yourself or get someone you know and trust to read the questions and you answer. I'd recommend that you do it yourself, with someone else and then with a real prospective or former customer. Once you do this you will be looking at life through the eyes of a true soul trader.

The first time I used this exercise was at one of my workshops where one of the attendees was a film maker. At the end I asked how useful it was. He replied: 'Very much so. I make romantic comedy films for American distribution for a largely female market. I realized it should be the guys in my movies that should take their clothes off, not the ladies!' He realized that he had been seeing his movies from his lens as a man not as the typical female viewer. Suddenly I realized that this was worth thousands of pounds for his business.

What have you learnt? Where are you at now? What can you apply? It may be useful for you to reflect on Chapter 1. If you're very passionate about X and Y, is that visible on your website? Is that there on your literature? If you're giving part of your profits to a cause or whatever, are you articulating that? If you set up your particular business to help X, Y and Z, are you saying that? Often at this point clients of mine realize that there are important achievements, features or benefits of their service that they are not articulating to customers that could be winning them business.

In sight, in mind, in heart

TABLE 2.2   In sight, in mind, in heart

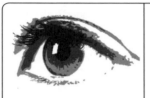	**In sight** *Step 1:* First of all potential customers need to be able to see you. You need to be visible. How will you find them and how will they find you? Without this first step nothing else can happen.
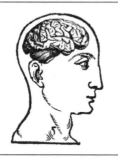	**In mind** *Step 2:* Being visible is a big step but it is not enough. Potential customers then need to have you in mind. To achieve this you need to understand them and their needs, and what you say needs to resonate with them and be relevant to them.
	**In heart** *Step 3:* This is the stage at which not only have you won your customers over but they hold you dear in their hearts. This is the stage it is essential you reach for the long haul. To achieve it you must truly care about your customers, and they will hold you dear. They will trust you, recommend you, refer others to you and be loyal to you. But for it to last you must also keep them in your sight, in mind and at heart.

Ultimately what you want is a strong robust business where customers love you and what you do. Many large and small businesses take their eye, mind and heart off their customers, customer relationships and customer service, and that makes customers fall out of love with them.

In sight

First of all you need to be in view. You need to be visible to your customers. How will you find your customers and how will they find you? Most soul traders gain most of their business through their contacts, networks, customer referral and other direct means of meeting potential customers. It is the most direct and often the least expensive way. Who is in your network? Does everyone in your network know what you're doing and how it can help them and those they know? Have you explained it in a way that they can relate to others? This is the theme that we will build on in Chapters 4 ('Cooperation') and 5 ('Conversations'). There are all sorts of other ways to be in view through networking, social networking, events, business organizations and so on. Are you out in the world virtually and physically? What are your competitors and others in your sector doing? What is right for you?

Raspinder is a young entrepreneur developing an online service for graduates setting up in business. He'd got very busy on creating his site, but was not asking graduates what they wanted or becoming visible, so our strategy has been to get him talking to students online and offline and to get him out from behind his computer at business, networking and student events and so on. He has joined and visited many of the websites. For the soul trader being literally visible is important – once people start to see your face regularly at events, online you start to be noticed.

Which ways could you be more visible? In Chapter 1 we learnt a little about Karen the recruitment consultant. Once Karen and I started working together I asked her about her visibility, and we identified industry events that she could attend, network at and possibly even speak at. Likewise there were specialist magazines for which she could write articles, sharing her expertise. Whilst she was a little unsure about the speaking, she realized that she could network more, follow up with more clients between pieces of work and attend more conferences. She has a niche area of recruitment, and merely attending a conference every quarter and networking effectively will boost her visibility. In this it is important to know your strength and style. Karen is good with people, and writing is something she's quite open to. She realized it is an area that may add to her visibility and credibility and would give her, as she described it, 'a voice' with which to talk about important issues in her industry and to her customers.

In mind

Once you are in sight you can be in mind. You can't achieve the latter until the former takes place. This sounds obvious, but I am amazed by the number of established business owners who do not have websites – or do not have good ones. I am also amazed how many business owners underutilize their network and contacts who could help them become more visible. But we will come on to that in more detail later. If we do not tell people what we are doing how can we come to their mind when they need our service? Whilst you're reading this, if certain people or opportunities come to mind, make a note of them and then explore how to act on it.

Being in mind is not quite as straightforward as it seems. Being in the mind of your potential client requires skill and insight. In this chapter we've started to explore how there is actually a lot of psychology involved with buying, which we will look at later. It goes far beyond what you are and what you sell. It is really about your customers and how they relate to what you do. Here are some aspects of being in mind:

I **Communicate:** You need to say something that is relevant, whether it's what you say (and show) on your website or business card or at an event or meeting. In most cases this means it needs to be clear, crisp and concise. The secret to this is to be warm, interested and interesting. You have to be yourself, or your potential customer will see through you.

2 **Connect:** What you say must resonate with your audience and what's important to them. This is why we have spent a lot of time looking at the world through your customers' eyes. A little homework on your customers will help – or simply asking them about themselves and their priorities.

3 **Convince:** Convincing is a 'click' that happens in the mind of the customer if you have been effective with steps 1 and 2. It is not about you trying to convince the customer. How often has a cold caller managed to convince you by labouring the point? In most instances all that kind of approach does is make you determined not to buy.

In other words, be it in person or in your promotions, you need to 'speak' to what it is that is important to your potential customer. We will look deeply at this relationship in Chapters 4 ('Cooperation') and 5 ('Conversations'). But, to set the scene, every customer has a conscious or unconscious set of concerns, aspirations and desires related to their life, the situation that they are in, and the service or product need that they have that you can satisfy. Now your service or product either meets that need or does not. Part of that is down to you. You should ensure your product actually does what it says on the tin and is of a good quality and standard; otherwise you should not be in business, or you need to work on the product until it meets the standard and then market it to your customers. Much of the rest of the job is to be able to communicate effectively and to reach your customer. Once your prospective customers believe that you understand them deeply then you will be in their mind. If the conditions are favourable they are likely to buy. If what you do at the event, online or in your leaflet really resonates they will be likely to buy.

In heart

The last stage of this is being in their heart. In order to be in your customer's heart, the customer really needs to love you and to love what you do. For that, customers may well need to have an experience of you. What is it we could do in order to get our customers into our hearts? How can we be in each other's hearts? Perhaps that means, depending on the nature of your service, that there are free samples. Perhaps you can give them a free consultation. Perhaps they can have a taster. Perhaps you can have a conversation with them. There may be all sorts of different ways, but we do need to get into their hearts, and this needs to be meaningful and very authentic.

Being in sight, heart and mind

Now that we've begun to explore things from our customer's point of view we can begin to look at how we need to engage with them. How is it that we're able to win business? How is it that we can win business very, very directly? Big businesses often spend huge sums of money on marketing, advertising, customer research and so on. As a small business owner or as an individual, you probably don't have that kind of luxury, but if you understand customers powerfully you can begin to market to them powerfully.

Know the numbers

Keep your mind on the money and your heart on the customers.

One of the biggest pitfalls for soul traders is not earning enough money to live on and to run a profitable business, or they may simply not spend enough time focusing on the money side of the business. This happens for a range of reasons. It may be that finance and figures are not your strong point; you may prefer the customer or creative parts of the business. You may have all sorts of social, ethical or spiritual views about money, capitalism, business and so on. In a way your views on these things are immaterial; unless you run a profitable business that is financially compliant you will be unable to sustain yourself, support your loved ones or make the difference that you want to make by running your business. I've made this mistake in the past, and it is counter-productive to everything you're looking to achieve. I only survived because the outgoings and costs of my business were relatively low. Otherwise I might not be writing this book!

It is essential that we see money in perspective. Money is simply the current form of exchange that we use for goods and services. It is an inanimate object, which is neither good nor bad; it is your relationship and actions with it that make it so. Throughout humankind's time on the planet we have used differing methods of transfer. First we bartered, then we used minerals and gems, then we fashioned coins and notes and plastic cards, and now we also use invisible digital transfers. It may even be the case that we'll return to bartering – and in fact in times of economic austerity that is what we do. Essentially nothing has changed; we are exchanging skills and resources sometimes – and later in the book I will highlight other ways of exchanging creatively and collaboratively.

As a soul trader you have the opportunity to be part of the movement that is positively changing our relationship to business, finance, debt, greed and selfishness by running a business that nourishes you and others. You have an opportunity to build a business that provides a 'wealth of possibilities' in whatever way you choose to interpret or redefine it.

Making a profit is only part of the story. It may take a month or more to be paid, and you may have large outgoings in the meantime, so even if you are making a profit on paper your business could go to the wall by not having enough cash to pay its bills, you, your staff and your suppliers. The key to your success is cash flow. See cash flow as the blood pumping through the veins of your business.

Sarah ran a successful travel business. She built it from scratch, from working in her home to setting up a team of staff and offices in the heart of London. At the start, her finances were straightforward, but as the business grew in terms of staff, costs, transactions and premises a small problem of not being good with figures turned into a large one of being overwhelmed. Unfortunately by the time she and I had the conversation and she decided to get further help it was too late: the business was in too much financial trouble.

As one business expert once put it to me, as a business owner you can delegate financial responsibility but you cannot abdicate it. The sad thing was that Sarah was a soul trader with a fantastic business that helped others and had scope to expand, but the fact that the finances were overlooked was like an iceberg that was not spotted.

Asking for help and developing the right team of support are among the key factors of being a successful business owner. It is also why we will specifically look at conversations and cooperation. The right conversation at the right time may have saved Sarah's business.

If you find finances difficult it's essential that you seek help via those you know and trust and through those with the expertise to help you. It may also help you to think about the 'numbers' in more inspiring ways. Relate the numbers to how you help people; relate your finances to the numbers of customers or projects you need to run a profitable business. There may well be spreadsheets and bills to look at, but once you are clear that it's actually about projects, people and products you'll advance as a soul trader.

In short, what it's crucial to know is how many customers and sales you need to run your business successfully – and the related costs of running your business and making those sales.

Figure 2.2 is a simple representation of money going out on the left (bills, costs, etc) and money coming in on the right (customers, products, projects). Some of these figures may be fixed, and some may vary. Perhaps the key aspect is the central funnel by which customers or work projects are coming in. This is where all the work you've already done in this chapter comes to life. If we work our way backwards from customers who have come through the funnel:

I **How many customer sales do you need or want per month?**
   Once you know the numbers you need and/or the combination (if you provide a range of services or goods) then focus on that number – or a higher number if you wish. Once people

FIGURE 2.2 Your finances

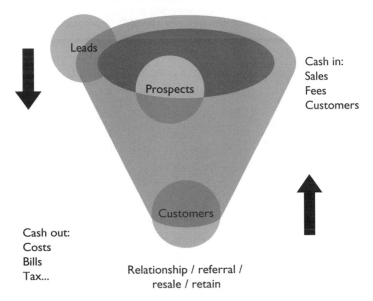

Leads

Cash in:
Sales
Fees
Customers

Prospects

Customers

Cash out:
Costs
Bills
Tax...

Relationship / referral /
resale / retain

are customers keep them in sight and in mind so that the relationship remains strong. How can you keep them dear so that they will return, refer and recommend? Remember to work out how much it actually costs you to produce your product or service and to gain and retain your various customers. You may find that some products and services have far lower production, promotional and services costs than others.

2 **What is the stage just before someone becomes your customer?** Is it a meeting, proposal, online enquiry or something else? How many of these does it take on average to convert into a customer or sale? If you are established, monitor this. If you are new, do the same! Let's imagine that one in three meetings, proposals or enquiries turns into a client. How many of these do you need in a month or a year? Focus your activity to generate those numbers. These are people who have you 'in mind', so how can you connect with them at heart? Could (should) you offer a 'test drive',

taster, trial, freebie or chat so that people can experience you and what you do? Choose what you give carefully so that it honours and values you rather than the opposite.

3 **What happens with 'hot prospects'?** This directly relates to the customer scenarios. What are the scenarios for your customers that are most likely to make them want and need you? Focus all your marketing activities on these people rather than 'anybody'. Many businesses spend huge amounts of money on lead generation and 'cold calling' that often delivers poorly. In Chapter 5 ('Conversations') I will share how you can change this by making 'warm calls', and in Chapter 6 ('Creativity') we will explore other ways that you can use your own magic to generate opportunities. With hot prospects the key thing is that you are 'in sight' and 'in mind'. Mindful of this, the rest of this book really looks at how you can develop the contacts, confidence and conversations to spot, create and gain these opportunities by operating from your heart.

To keep your funnel flowing you may need a pool of new leads from which to identify prospects. Where will they come from: networking, referrals, shows, exhibitions, meetings, online marketing or other areas?

The essential questions

1 How much money do you need to live on and to break even in business?

2 How much money do you seek to make this year, next year and the year after in turnover – before costs and tax – and in your personal profit after costs and tax?

3 On average how many sales or customers does that equate to per month and year?

4 What specific actions are needed to reach those goals, and what are the challenges?

5 What evidence, research and assumptions are those figures based on?

6 Looking again at those figures, what are a) realistic, b) optimistic and c) pessimistic sales figures for the next 12 months, and what would they mean to you and your business?

7 What are your main products and services? How are they priced? What are all the costs involved? Which are the most lucrative? Which incur the most costs? Which involve the most hard work? Which are most dear to your heart and to your customers?

Depending on your knowledge and expertise and the nature and complexity of your business some of these questions may be easy or tough, but it is essential look at them so that you can run a profitable business. It also need not be daunting if you are ready to reach out and develop connections and resourcefulness that can help, which is what this book is all about. So the central question for you is: What knowledge, support and systems do you have to understand and manage your business finances, and what additional help, knowledge and skills do you need?

These are exactly the kinds of calculations Robert needed to make for his IT, accounting and software business. When I met Robert he was a consultant making a good living, but he wanted to take his business to the next stage. He developed clarity, as we did in Chapter 1, and he set his sights on new customers, as we have done. Now, three years on, he has about eight staff and major companies as clients. Shrewdly, as his business started to grow, he chatted to Heather, a business operations and finance specialist, to calculate differing scenarios of sales, cost and profit so he could make the best decisions about how to move ahead without overstretching himself. He recognized that, as his business grew, so too would resource demands, staff costs and some other costs, and that financial forecasting would need more care. This was important, even though he personally is good with figures.

This may be the scenario you're in, or perhaps your scenario is more straightforward, like that of our recruitment specialist Karen. In her case she just needed to clarify the types and number of new clients she needed to bring on board. Karen is lucky in that her business 'numbers' are easier to manage, and the main focus is winning the new customers.

Staying in love

It is not enough that customers fall in love with you and what you do. It is very important that they continue to feel that way. And as with any relationship that will last and be enriching to both parties it requires love, kindness, respect and attention.

You know how to do this because – returning to where we began this chapter – you know what it is like to be a customer. You know how it is to be neglected by a business, and you know what it is like to be hounded by one too. What do you want as a customer? As your business grows, ask your customers – they will tell you how they want to be served, communicated with and so on.

Warm service and kindness as far as I am concerned are essential in any business, and this must be genuine. This means that anyone who is working for or representing your business must deliver to the same standards. In the event of complaints it is important that you have procedures in place, and depending on the nature of your business there may well be additional standards, ethics and levels of compliance to meet; again, it is your responsibility to find that out. As your business develops, expands or diversifies there will be fresh customer issues and needs to be met, and all of this highlights the significance of cooperation and why we will be looking at it more closely.

All businesses and business owners find their own unique ways of developing that loving relationship with their customers. Some use lots of incentives, offers, prizes, competitions, surveys and feedback to keep customers informed and to improve services. Many utilize customer participation and testimonials. There is rich value in all of these. But all of these tools are just tools. Good as they may be, if customers feel your company is just going through the motions or simply trying to do whatever it takes to entice them these methods may well backfire.

Apple stay in love with their customers through the quality of their products, the technology, the design aesthetic that they and their customers share – and continual innovation. John Lewis use the power of their customer service, their excellent staff and knowledge, and the guarantee that they give. They may not have a regular dialogue with their customers, but the customers know the company will be reliable. The nature of your relationship and the regularity of contact may well vary, as with all relationships. What's important is the love, warmth, respect, trust, support – and equally the space that you give each other to a degree that is right.

Your business will be shaped around this 'dance' between you and your customers – it's where your clarity around your unique service, story, product and mission meets your customers' needs. It's a relationship that should make customers come to you, stay with you, refer others to you and come back to you – time after time. And it is your love of what you do and those you serve – and your attentiveness to them – that means the dance works wonderfully. As with any dance there may well be stumbles and slip-ups, but strong partnerships will adjust. Soul traders will take these things in their stride.

But wherever you are on the journey it is likely that it will require courage, and that is precisely what we are going to focus on now.

SUMMARY

1 Do you know what you want? If so, now it's all about
   your customers.

2 Your customers won't care about you or what you do until you care
   about them.

3 Clarify the precise scenarios in which customers might want or
   need you.

4 See life through your customers' eyes: ensure your products and
   promotion match.

5 Explore how you can be in sight and mind: think hot prospects;
   give short test drives.

6 Know the numbers that you need, and identify the help and support
   you require.

7 Keep your customers at heart and stay in touch.

COURAGE

Utilize your inner strength

There's but one true act of courage in life – becoming who you are.

There's no question that courage will be necessary throughout your journey to build a successful and fulfilling business as a soul trader. Where is it that you're going to find that courage?

There are many challenges in starting up, finding the right people to help you, gaining and maintaining customers, and balancing business with your personal life. There will be challenges in meeting the differing demands and needs within your business: operational, organizational, technical, prioritizing and marketing. There will be all sorts of financial and economic challenges as the business landscape changes.

Some of these you may have foreseen, such as finding the suppliers, setting up systems, and marketing and promoting to win customers. There may be challenges you have not anticipated, such as an internet or database crash that could incapacitate your business for days or weeks. There may be problems that you should plan for, such as your main customer suddenly going, leaving a big hole in your finances. There may be challenges with a business partner or with friends and family. You may want or need to diversify, expand, change your business or price structure, take on staff or outsource work. All of these things will require courage.

This is why it's so important that you run your business from your heart. The clearer you are and the more deeply you are connected to what your passion, mission and values are, the more aware and able to make decisions and resilient you will be on the journey.

There are many reasons why so many businesses start and fail quickly. Lack of planning, research and skills, and limited resources play a huge part – but passion, courage and conviction play just as big a part. These are things that nobody else can give you. You must (re)discover them within yourself. This chapter of the book will help you – and these challenges that emerge along your path will push you to find courage.

The exercise in Table 3.1 will help you become clearer about your-self and your magic and will help your courage and confidence. It is subtle but often profound:

♥ **List three people who inspire you most in life.** They may be living or have passed on, famous or known only to you and the select few. They may be historical figures or modern-day ones. They may be close to you, such as a friend, family member or colleague, or people you have never met. But I want one of them to be someone involved in business or enterprise in some way, shape or form. It may be a traditional business or a form of entertainment, sport or the arts where the person has been enterprising. Including someone with a business connection brings an added degree of insight and relevance to the journey you are on – regardless of whether the business is similar to yours.

♥ **Write down three qualities that you admire in each of these three people.** In other words, why is it you admire them? What are the specific skills, attributes and gifts that they have and utilize? Try to be as specific as you can be.

♥ **In what way do you share each quality in each person? Write down an example.** This may seem tough. You may be thinking 'Rasheed, these people are remarkable and have done remarkable things, and I don't have any of their qualities.' But there will be a degree to which you share that quality, virtue, skill or life value – even in a small way.

TABLE 3.1 Tapping into your inspiration

Qualities I admire	How I've demonstrated these qualities
Person 1:	
1.	1.
2.	2.
3.	3.
Person 2:	
1.	1.
2.	2.
3.	3.
Person 3:	
1.	1.
2.	2.
3.	3.

I remember an occasion at my British Library workshop where I invited delegates to do this exercise. One attendee was a trade union rep and starting her own business. She identified the three people she admired and the qualities that she admired in each person, but she was really struggling with how she had those qualities. I asked her to tell me one of the people she had picked and one of the qualities. She named the person and said that a quality was 'They stood up for what they believed in.' I said 'Could it be that through your work of being a trade union rep you're constantly standing up for things that you believe in?' She replied: 'Oh yes, I'd never thought of it like that.' She was so close to her role that she could not immediately see it from this perspective. You too may be blind to your own magic. If so, ask some people whom you know, love, respect and trust.

I'm constantly amazed at how subtle yet powerful this is. On the surface level you may think that this exercise is all about those extraordinary and ordinary people who have made an impact on your life and in the world. To an extent this is true, but it's really about you and your magic. You've chosen the people you admire. You selected them because their values are important to you and are ones you live by already, or they are there in you, below the surface, underutilized, and you need to bring them to the fore and use them more.

It might well be the case that they have been courageous or have stood up for what they believed and that *you* need to do that a little bit more. There are hints and tips that will be extremely useful here for you. A delegate at one of my events had recently given up a highly paid job in the City. I asked him who inspired him. He said it was a family member who had died through illness. I asked him to name one of the qualities he admired in her. He replied 'Her courage.' I asked him 'How do you have courage?' He replied 'I don't have it.' I asked him 'Could it be that you have had courage in giving up a highly paid job to follow your heart and to set up a business?' Slightly surprised he said 'Oh yes – and I was inspired by her courage to start up on my own.' It was a powerful realization that helped strengthen that courage.

Your virtual mentors

From now on I'm going to refer to the three people you have selected as your *virtual mentors*. I invite you to adopt them as your virtual mentors so that you can draw on their insights, wisdom and courage. You may want to add one or two more people to this list. If so, it's good to have a blend of those who are business-savvy and those who are world-wise.

Write down three pieces of advice they'd give you to help you achieve your life and business goals. Imagine they know your whole life story: your dreams and aspirations; your strengths, gifts, talents, weaknesses and shortcomings; and what stage you're at. Imagine they have been following your progress through this book and the exercises you've completed (or not). Some virtual mentors will be strategic, logical, business-savvy and process-driven and may give you specific advice on how to move forward on business management operation, finance and marketing. Others will be more spiritual or philosophical and offer inspirational and motivational insights.

So what does all that information tell you? Maybe it's that you need to trust, focus, plan or research. Perhaps it's that you need to be brave, be innovative, seek out specific expertise, learn new skills or utilize your resources. Meditate on the advice that you have. Combine it with all the insights you've already gained, including your customer insight.

There may be commonalities between your virtual mentors. They may have had fears, setbacks, doubts and doubters, made mistakes and had to persist and believe in themselves and their dreams. There are often many layers to the advice to consider. How did your virtual mentors progress? What can you learn and apply?

Ultimately the question is: Are you going to act on this advice – which actually comes from your deeper self – or are you going to ignore it?

You may wish to seek out real mentors to help you with your personal or business development. Some people have mentors who

TABLE 3.2   Advice from my virtual mentors

Pieces of advice they'd give me
Virtual mentor 1:
1.
2.
3.
Virtual mentor 2:
1.
2.
3.
Virtual mentor 3:
1.
2.
3.

are very business related. Some people have mentors who are far more their personal and spiritual mentors, and many have a broad range.

David's virtual mentors

David runs a market intelligence consultancy that helps businesses understand their customers and enter new marketplaces through this research. He's also passionate about his family and is keen to make his own contribution to the world through supporting international development charities. We exchanged some coaching sessions for his marketing consultancy. Like many soul traders, David is quite selfless and often puts others' needs ahead of his. We set very specific financial goals to raise his fees, and to allow more time for his wife and the couple's application to adopt a son. He particularly needed the courage to charge more, so we selected three 'virtual mentors' to help: Sir Richard Branson for business advice; the Dalai Lama for guidance on life balance; and Bob Geldof, whose 'Give us your money' mantra would remind David to ensure he raised the money he needed. It has started to pay dividends. He and his wife now have a son and a daughter, and the family have all moved to the country to enjoy a higher quality of life. Meanwhile David has stabilized his business and raised his fees, and he's getting involved in an international trade project. All this emerged from inner courage.

Self-belief and your personal journey

Over the years I have addressed thousands of people at talks, and wanting more confidence, courage, motivation, self-belief, determination, inspiration and focus are always top of delegates' lists of wants. I often get people to share their story, passion and mission. The energy in the room rises, and delegates become fascinated and captivated in a way that they would not if they had talked about just the business. This sharing brings more clarity, drive and courage. You may think that you are simply developing a product, becoming your own boss or expanding your business to the next level. You are not. You are doing something much more. You are on your own unique, magical journey.

The journey is slightly or very different for us all, and it can be a lonely, frustrating and challenging one. It can also often be exciting and natural. But the nature of the journey will require you to develop within yourself and with your business – whether that business starts and remains as being just you, or whether you need to attract and bring on board others, or indeed whether you already have partners, staff or associates on board.

I remember travelling to the Lake District area of England to visit Steve, an accomplished trainer who worked with senior managers. He invited me to climb a few hills that he used to coach these high achievers. As we reached the summit of one of the highest hills, after regaining my breath I said 'Wow, this is great. You're very adventurous. I'm so unadventurous.' Steve picked up on it immediately and said 'Actually, I think you're very adventurous', and said that all I had achieved as a coach and speaker and following my own path was because I was courageous and adventurous. So sometimes we do not see our courage or magic until it is pointed out. Sometimes we call it by another name.

Courage starting a business

Starting up can be enormously challenging. It can involve emotional and lifestyle upheavals as well as retraining, gaining new skills, product development, market research and gathering the right expertise and support.

For the soul trader there is often no choice but to start. In my own case, life was moving me in that direction. After 10 years in my first job in PR and media relations I had been made redundant. I fought and resisted it, but actually it was great for me and I did well financially out of it. That said, I was young – and naive – and spent most of it. But I was not entirely naive. I vowed never to work full time again. I realized that, however loyal I might be to an employer, the employer might not be able to be loyal to me. I also wanted to explore my own passion. Mine was a gradual movement. I worked part time to pursue my singing career. Working part time wasn't easy; finding the part-time posts in my field as a single man wasn't easy. 'Why do you want to work part time? You don't have childcare responsibilities' seemed to be the unsaid reaction. My singing led me to meet other singers and performers who had struggled in their careers. This developed my interest in coaching. At the same time I volunteered for Samaritans. Parallel to this I found myself on my own spiritual journey of self-discovery. Meanwhile my part-time roles were becoming more challenging. I was effectively forced out of one of the jobs, and there were two or three phases of being unemployed when I had to support myself through my fast-evaporating redundancy settlement. I found myself retraining as a coach and starting to work as a coach with singers. This was a big decision, as it pretty much took the remainder of my savings.

Once I was trained as a coach – and in fact whilst I was training – I dipped my toe in the water of coaching. I coached a few singers, some work colleagues and a former boss. I was honing my craft, but I didn't quite have the courage to make the full leap. Eventually the part-time role I was doing again became difficult – and major changes and differences of opinion with management made me realize I had to leave. Events, together with where I was travelling, edged me out the door.

I 'guesstimated' that I needed three months' salary to find my feet and get myself up and running. The first few months and indeed years were not easy financially, but at last I was following my heart. People often set a budget and a timeframe by which to make the business a success or if it's not been met find a job.

This kind of story is echoed again and again by other soul traders. Susan started her business following a long successful career as an executive PA working for senior managers. However, it was far from easy and was not all a matter of choice. Susan is a mum and had always enjoyed jogging to keep fit. In a short space of time she found herself seriously unwell and was diagnosed with a brain tumour. It was devastating, and she had to re-evaluate everything.

She realized that she could not and did not want to work in the same full-on way again. She regained her health and set up as a virtual assistant providing support to small business owners. She became passionate about helping others who also wanted the flexibility of being virtual assistants, and she built up a team of associates. Her dedication led her to win the title of Virtual Assistant of the Year. She is now writing a book to help others start up and working with me as my part-time executive assistant. Several years on, Susan's new challenges are about taking the business to the next level and generating a good income for herself and her family. She says:

> The biggest challenge has been to continue to do it – despite what others say. For me courage is also about looking at the bigger picture and believing in yourself. People say and think that coping with a brain tumour took courage. I had no choice but to have the operation. For me the real challenge is to get up every morning and to keep moving forward.

Diana's business emerged from courage. Soon after having one of her children she too fell ill. Following a series of operations she was diagnosed with ME, a chronic fatigue illness. She was determined to get better, and slowly she did. She developed an interest in hypnotherapy and trained as a clinical hypnotherapist and later in reiki. Her courage led her into business, and she now helps others overcome their own fears and phobias through her business.

An alternative life

Steve is an author, and co-director of Alternatives, which runs talks from leading spiritual and personal development speakers. He grew up in the 1960s, when you were expected to get a job, raise a family, work hard, retire and hopefully spend your remaining years relaxing or doing a hobby that you loved. Steve did get a job, raise a family and work hard. However, in his thirties he felt compelled to go on a journey of self-discovery. Steve told me:

> While that may be common now, 25 years ago taking an interest in self, personal and spiritual development and exploring things like meditation, energy and healing was not that common. This journey did take a huge amount of courage. After 20 years doing a fixed career the thought of resigning to follow my heart was both scary and compelling. Now looking back I have no regrets leaving my old career to follow my sense of passion, inspiration and true calling. The past 12 years have been the most amazing time in my working life. And it seems to get better each year. I have written four books in that time, travelled, and worked around the UK and Europe.

The journey led him to help build Alternatives, which has helped thousands of people along their life paths. Steve says: 'For me courage is the ability to take a step forward whilst staying in touch with my truth, my heart, my vision. Courage is feeling the fear and if it feels right doing it anyway!'

Finding yourself and your space and being true to yourself

Finding yourself and your unique space in the business world can take time and courage. In my own case, once I had qualified as a coach I had to find my own identity and my own style to stand out. Even then there were a few thousand coaches in the UK. My training was excellent, but as I began coaching I felt there was something missing: what I call the 'intangible invisible' things that were important such as trust, acceptance, energy and flow. I needed to incorporate those into my approach. Now coaching is largely about setting and achieving goals, and I was a bit nervous about how I would marry in the new ideas. Would this stuff seem too 'fluffy' for the business clients I was starting to meet? Fortunately I've always been quite intuitive, and I knew I had to go with it. I found myself writing every day, and my first book, which I later self-published as *The Gift of Inner Success*, encapsulated these themes.

Around this time I produced my first audio talk, called 'Create your ideal life'. It was quite a traditional tool, fine but quite generic and 'safe' – I wasn't standing out. Again I felt that something was missing. I then wrote the sleeve notes, which came out as a stream of consciousness. They summarized the essence of what would become my approach. I felt in many ways that the sleeve notes were more powerful than the audio talk! I had to have the courage to stand by it and also to continue to follow the path that was unfolding. The momentum carried me to produce my second audio talk, 'Become who you are'. This was my arrival: a semi-meditative talk and invitation to listeners to follow their heart and find their way back to the core. But again at first I was quite nervous about how these two differing aspects – the practical and the spiritual – sat together. It required courage. It required trust. It required all the themes that were emerging for me and in my work. I had to embrace them. And I am glad that I did, for it is these things that have given me my unique edge as a coach in my field. It is these things that have drawn customers to me, and I use 'Become who you are' as my tagline to this day.

This journey to find yourself personally and your space in business is not something you can fake. In many ways a business is not created; it is born. It naturally emerges from you. Like the birth of a child it may be triumphant and traumatic, and it may emerge as a result of two forces coming together. Tended carefully it will develop naturally and magically – often even beyond your own knowing and comprehension. Likewise the business that emerges has a life and magic of its own. The key is to trust and be true.

And so for many a soul trader courage is about being true to you. In my own case being true to myself is how my business is run. I run my business by listening to my heart. It is run on being still, silent and true to what emerges. It is about stepping back from even being Rasheed Ogunlaru the coach, speaker and author, and just watching, trusting and observing what is unfolding. I've realized that this has always been the case. It was true for me when I pursued singing and performing as a living. It was true throughout my previous career in press and PR. I still have my doubts, but I listen to my heart and follow it, and it has made my life and work richer than I can put into words.

The courage that you need within your business may be a reflection of the courage that you need to embrace the challenges that are going on in your life. The two are interconnected. In fact your business probably is the manifestation of all that is going on in your life – your unique life.

For you this courage may manifest itself in many ways. It may be about making big decisions like whether to leave your job, take on your first employee or move your operations abroad. It might be smaller things like letting go of a task and finding someone else to do it, asking for help with marketing or admin or going on a new course. Or it may be simply changing the wording about you on your website to make it more bold, forthcoming and able to 'sell' your accomplishments.

There will be times running your business when nothing works. All of the books, tools, techniques, courses, training and business models may fall flat. There will be times when the local or global economy may take an unforeseen turn. These are the times when your courage needs to be at its most powerful.

Seven courage issues starting out

1 Giving yourself the space to explore what *you* want.

2 Having the courage to follow your heart and beliefs.

3 Having the courage to ask people for help and getting expert help.

4 Having the courage to speak out loud and say this is who I am and what I do.

5 Having the courage to put your toe in the water and test your idea out.

6 Having the courage to put in the time and effort to develop yourself and your business.

7 Having the courage to change things if they are not working.

These themes relate to the ground we've covered in Chapters 1 ('Clarity') and 2 ('Customers') and in this chapter, so you may already be well on your way.

Pleasure and pain, trials and rewards

Foluke runs an online magazine and resource for women of colour called *Precious Online*. She told me: 'Since I was six years old I spent all my pocket money on magazines. I vowed that when I got older I would launch a magazine aimed at women like me.' True to her vow she set up the *Precious Online* magazine and the Precious Awards to celebrate the achievements of black and ethnic minority women. Today it receives around 80,000 visitors per month. Foluke told me a bit about the courage involved:

It's been a struggle from the very start. When I launched, the web was in its early stages in the UK, so many people just didn't understand the idea of having an online magazine. Access to finance is always a struggle. I've never received any funding or taken out a loan and have invested any profits back into the business. Finding the right people to work with is a challenge. I am a Northerner [from the North of England], so I think I have this innate stubbornness in me that refuses to accept defeat!

Foluke's courage has paid off; she received the MBE for her accomplishments:

I was totally shocked, so shocked that when the Cabinet Office rang to tell me I thought it was a prank call and put the phone down on them. Despite the various challenges and ups and downs I have faced, I would always say to someone looking to start their own business to go for it. You will always be wondering 'What if...?' I would also advise writing a very short business plan, surrounding yourself with people who genuinely want the best for you and getting yourself a coach.

Courage growing a business

I met Graham when he was on the journey, as he put it, 'from being a consultant to being an entrepreneur'. He had established Think Productive, a business to help other businesses become effective and organized. For this he knew he needed a strategy, belief, to bring on board staff and to create a business model that would work and move him from being a one-person business to a scalable business. Through planning and hard work in little over a year he had moved from being a single-person business to having four staff and an office. Graham says:

There have been some moments on my journey over the last couple of years that have required courage, but I don't particularly feel courageous! What I've always had with Think Productive was a very clear vision of what I wanted to create. So when I've been forced to take financial and personal risks to make stuff happen it's usually been possible not because of any courage, confidence or 'gung-ho-ness' I possess, but because my mind is so focused on that end vision, which gives me the guidance I need to act on. So I wouldn't call it courage as much as to call it focus.

Graham says: 'It's easier to be courageous if you're focused. If you have a clear sense of what point you want to get to, how you're going to do it and whether the odds are stacked in your favour or against you, you can much more easily make decisions about how to act. You won't always be right, though!' As a coach and mentor I have been continually impressed by how Graham has embraced the challenges and found the strength to forge ahead by building his business from his heart.

Growing your business may in fact not always be about taking on staff or offices. One such expert I've coached is a Harley Street doctor who specializes in weight loss. He wants to remain a one-person business, but he wants more 'A' list clients, a waiting list and possibly to add a few products. He is on track. He's had some celebrity clients, has established a niche female client group – and has written a book. For this doctor, courage will take a new form: the courage to put himself in the limelight on TV and radio and in the press – something he has shied away from in the past. He has begun to expand his comfort zone by giving talks and writing articles.

If, as for the doctor, your business growth isn't necessarily about taking on staff and expanding offices then it may well be that courage for you will include broadening your networks and raising your profile, speaking, writing and utilizing various media. If so, Chapters 4 ('Cooperation'), 5 ('Conversations') and 6 ('Creativity') will be especially valuable.

Seven common challenges for growing your business

Here are some of the most common challenges you will face as a soul trader:

1 giving yourself time and space to review and improve your dream;

2 asking for help, saying 'yes' and 'no', and changing what's not working;

3 taking on staff, virtual assistants or business partners – especially the first;

4 developing management skills, delegating effectively and letting go;

5 finding the business shape and model that work for you and your business;

6 raising finance and finding the right resources for your business growth;

7 increased logistics, managing time and risks, and entering new markets.

All these things are about knowing, exploiting, testing and expanding your comfort zones, expertise and capacity. Keep these themes in mind as you progress through this book. The remaining chapters will prompt you to address those that may affect you.

Business nightmares and new horizons

There is often a perception that, when the business is up, running and growing, you will have made it. There's also a myth that, once you have made money, your money problems will go away. Sometimes it simply means that there are differing money problems: more staff to pay; bigger investment projects to undertake; higher bills to meet. Sometimes you may face more competition or criticism in the marketplace. Sometimes there will be more challenge balancing a successful business and having a personal and social life. Sometimes you may find the business grows to a size and in ways that you didn't anticipate. Sometimes you may find yourself asking yourself new questions about what you want. Sometimes life, market and competitive forces and economic events may shake you from your plans. Sometimes, as we'll see in Rachel's case, a combination of these things may happen that will test your courage. It is at these times that returning to your core, your passion and your purpose will be vital, and events may take you and your business in new directions.

Rachel Elnaugh made her name setting up the innovative business Red Letter Days, which provided experiences as special gifts and corporate incentives. She then became one of the first 'dragons' on the first series of the popular BBC1 show *Dragons' Den*. I met Rachel when she became a mentor at the British Library's Business and IP Centre. I heard her speak at one of the Library's Inspiring Entrepreneur events called Business Nightmares, based on her book of the same name, where she openly shared many of the challenges she'd encountered setting up and ultimately having to sell Red Letter Days. The difficulties of seeing a multimillion-pound business slip through her hands, raising five children and facing public battles must have been remarkable. As I listened to Rachel give her talk I was struck by her honesty. We were lucky enough to have a mentoring and coaching session together. It was clear that there was another, more potent kind of courage that Rachel was having to find: the courage to be herself and to forge a new path – the courage to embrace her own journey as a soul trader.

Here's what Rachel says about her journey and courage:

At the time I was going through the Red Letter Days meltdown and associated media humiliation I really did think it was the end of my life. I'd lost the business I had devoted 16 years to, along with all the money that went with it, and I was certain that no one would ever want to have anything to do with me again. But looking back I now realize that this meltdown was essential in bringing me on to my soul path. Since Red Letter Days crashed in 2005 I have been on my own journey of personal development and have been open to all sorts of coaches, mentors and transformational experiences.

However it was a session with Rasheed in 2011 which truly changed my life. I was telling him about the 'Definite Chief Aim Statement' I had created after reading Think and Grow Rich *by Napoleon Hill, which stated 'To generate £10 million cash at bank by 31 December 2012 through inspiring, motivating and empowering others to achieve personal fulfilment and success'. Rasheed asked me what I would do when the money arrived. I hadn't actually stopped to think about why I needed £10 million before! It was always just a magic figure for me – as that would have been the amount I would have created from Red Letter Days had we floated the company. So after a little thought I told him 'To end all of my mentoring programmes so I could travel the world, learn under all the best empowerment teachers of our time, then bring all the best bits back and assimilate/communicate them in a way that made it really easy for everyone to understand and learn from.' To which Rasheed replied 'So why don't you do that now?' I realized in that moment that I had been delaying my happiness by pushing it into the future. It was that meeting that gave me the inspiration to do just that – to help market and promote evolutionaries, change-makers and heart-centred thought leaders, which is now manifesting in an elegant and magical way. There is a great saying: 'Whatever you do, or dream you can, begin it. Boldness has genius and power and magic in it', which now resides on my office wall. I can honestly say that session with Rasheed was like walking through a doorway that has led me into a completely new and completely fulfilling life where success, money and love are all now flowing. Thank you, Rasheed.*

If like Rachel you have been in business for some time and have seen it from its highs and lows, the next phase of your journey may have a different perspective. It may well be about that journey to your heart. It may well be about simply operating your business from your heart. When I met Paul, a business owner in the building industry, he had run a successful business in the past. He was now building a new business with a couple of business associates. But somewhere along the journey he had lost his confidence. He told me that he was struggling to motivate his sales team and, to a degree, himself. I asked him how he had managed to sell in the past. He said he had done it by being himself. He likened it to how his father had helped him learn to ride a bike with a gentle, supportive hand. He realized that this gentle, supportive hand is all he needed to apply to his team – and to himself. So that's what he found the courage to do – to step back and just offer a supportive hand. It worked. After successfully building the company he asked himself again what he wanted. He took the courageous decision – he needed a break and wanted to spend more time on his wife and kids and explore new things, so he sold his stake in the company. Stepping away from your dream to find a new path takes courage.

The attitude of an athlete

Whatever your business you need to develop the attitude of an athlete to flourish:

- ♥ Study your field.
- ♥ Master your craft.
- ♥ Gather the right team.
- ♥ Know when to work and when to rest.
- ♥ Win and keep supporters.
- ♥ Keep your eye on your competitors.
- ♥ Give 100 per cent.
- ♥ Run your own race.

So again I ask: how big is it that you dream? If you seek to be an Olympic athlete there's only going to be one gold medallist every four years. There might well be injury, and somebody else might win the race. How hard are you prepared to work? Are you prepared to put in the practice week in and week out? Do you have a top-flight team and coach? How will you face the competition and conduct yourself before, during and outside the race?

The exercise in Table 3.3 will help you meditate on the answers and help you on the next phase of the journey.

TABLE 3.3   Thinking about the challenges

1.	What are the three main challenges that face you now?
2.	What mindset and beliefs do you need to face those challenges?
3.	How will you and your business need to be and act to meet the challenges?
4.	What specific resources do you need to meet these challenges?
5.	What staff, support and expertise do you need (paid for, hired and/or free)?

From fear to flow

The courage required by the soul trader was beautifully described by Donald, who initially came to me because his mind was racing with all sorts of personal challenges that were holding him back in business. He described his situation as like 'hanging on to a branch by the riverbank' while everything was flowing by. He felt opportunities were flowing by. We had begun to explore how he could embrace life, let go, and flow with the opportunities. He now sees himself as being the river. When you start to go with the flow and start accepting, many of the blocks clear. This is where Steve, the graphic designer we met in Chapter 1, is at. Steve needs to embrace his years of experience, find the courage to let go of his past setbacks, decide his direction and flow with it.

Leon is a film maker with a dream of setting up a business to support creative artists. He is one of the few to have made a film about the Dalai Lama, when he followed him for a year. Leon works full time in editing and has a young family, and his wife has just set up a business. He has a clear vision, and is now finding the courage to make that transition gradually. Leon told me his courage has come from the film itself and using it to attract those contacts who might help him, including myself.

Wherever you are at with your business, cooperation – forging the right relationships – will be essential. So now that we have developed the clarity, become clearer about our customers and rediscovered our courage we are ready to develop the magic cooperation to build our business by heart.

SUMMARY

1 Know why you're running your business and always have it in mind.
2 Remember what your skills and talents are and work from them.
3 Adopt virtual mentors for confidence – and seek out real ones as needed.
4 Find your unique style and path in your business; it becomes your unique selling point.
5 Know that doubts, fears and challenges are a natural part of the journey.
6 Know when it's time to diversify, change, consolidate or expand.
7 Adopt the attitude of an athlete; study your field, master your craft, and build your team.

COOPERATION

Boost your business
through relationships

*It's easy for all the branches of a tree – which shake so differently
in the breeze – never to wake and see they're interrelated,
interdependent and ultimately one at the root.*

Everything is related

Nothing happens without cooperation. The bus driver would not
stop at the bus-stop. People would not let each other on and off.

Nothing would be agreed or achieved in the workplace. Products would never arrive at the shops. The soul trader understands this and never takes it for granted.

You've already covered a huge amount of ground: You have become clear about who you are and what's really important. You have gained a deeper insight into your customers' mindsets and lives, and you have reconnected to your own inspiration and your courage. From this base the rest of the book is about building on all of this so that your business can blossom in all the ways that are relevant to you, be it increasing customer numbers, becoming more visible in your market, raising profits, new opportunities, taking on staff, expanding your business or gaining new leads.

This chapter explores how everything is ultimately about relationships, and if we are all interconnected you can use the power of building strong personal relationships to access the support, expertise, markets and opportunities that you need and seek. But in order to achieve this you must focus on building the relationship and not the sale.

Wherever you are at, cooperation is key. You may be a millionaire, but if you are unable to keep relationships cordial at home and agree with your partner who will pick up the children then your home and business life will become chaotic. You may have the best invention ever, but unless you are able to access and build relationships with the suppliers and stockists your brilliant invention will never reach market. If you are not likeable, your business is in big trouble, and staff and customers will leave – or never come to you.

At the same time everyone in business is in transition. Every business needs something – be it skills and expertise, contacts, suppliers, new customers or anything else. This means that the scope and opportunity for cooperation, and what may spring from it is vast.

Whilst writing this chapter alone, during one week I launched a website, video, and coaching initiative with a magazine and drinks company. On any given day I'm cooperating with clients, potential clients, contacts, marketing specialists, my virtual executive assistant – the list goes on. Every one of these relationships needs to be honoured, respected, served and appreciated. Without them there would have been no website, video, publicity, customers or income. If I nurture each relationship, all sorts of new opportunities might unfold in the future – but only when I stop to see it.

Cooperation is about the dance that must take place between you and everyone in your personal and business life. It's born of necessity and desire – but not always at the same time. For your business really to flourish to its full potential you need to know your own worth and you have to appreciate the value of others. This is extremely important, so I say it again: *you have to know your own worth and that of others.* This is not just in financial terms. You need to recognize your gifts and potential. I often have to remind even very 'accomplished' and wealthy clients of their worth so that they can fully exploit it and enjoy it. Often soul traders have limited resources, and so cooperation is vital.

Most specifically, as a small business you are likely to need:

- ♥ expertise to help start, sustain and grow your business;
- ♥ leads, introductions and contacts to gain more business;
- ♥ staff, partners, associates or supporters to operate and deliver your business;
- ♥ good relationships in your home and personal life.

Achieving your life and business goals through cooperation requires skill and care, conversations and creativity, which is why Chapters 5 ('Conversations') and 6 ('Creativity') follow – these aspects are linked and intertwine with cooperation. In my case every opportunity I have gained in my entire career since I was 18 has been born of utilizing these things, and in most cases I have had little or no money with which to 'bargain'.

So let's build on and forge strong relationships for you. As the word indicates, cooperation is not about *me, me, me.* The 'dance' is about developing powerful win–win scenarios for all – with

TABLE 4.1   10 common reasons for cooperating and collaborating

These are in no particular order and often have considerable crossover:	
1.	To access new skills, expertise and experience for your business.
2.	To access new customers, markets and opportunities.
3.	To boost your profile and visibility.
4.	To become bigger, stronger and more robust or scalable.
5.	To win or deliver bigger, more prestigious or more lucrative projects or contracts.
6.	To gain support, friendship, shared values or mentoring.
7.	To offer a wider range of products and services.
8.	To reduce the competition.
9.	To share costs or the 'burden' and/or to free up time and resources.
10.	To gain reputation and affiliation with a company or cause to benefit you or others.

genuine understanding, connectivity, reciprocity and respect. All these ingredients must be present; once overlooked or taken for granted, the relationship – business or personal – will wither and die.

If you're stuck right now, it may be that the support you need is absent or stagnant. The cooperation between you and your customers, contacts, staff and suppliers may not be in place or working. These relationships need to be not only in place but rich and earnest. If your relationships are rich, your life and business will be rich.

You can't achieve your goals on your own. Globally, nations and markets are interlinked; a market crash on one side of the world can have a knock-on effect on the other side of the world and pretty much everywhere in between. So if entire countries are not self-sufficient how is it that you can be? Even the most 'individual' 100-metres athlete requires a team: coaches, nutritionists, an agent, a manager, physios and fans, all playing a part in the process.

What's more, it is true that the life you seek has a lot to do with the company you keep. You need the right star team with the right skills – and in the right positions. Are the people in your life and business up to scratch?

Desire, fear and relationships

To build your business through strong relationships it's wise to understand the human condition and our drivers.

FIGURE 4.1   What life is about

Desire

Relationships

Fear

Life – as we experience it – is essentially about three things: desire; relationships; and fear. We experience ourselves in relation to others, objects and the world around us. Everything has a relationship to everything else:

- ♥ **You:** Who are you? What is it that you desire and fear? How do you relate and feel about yourself, your business, life and the world? Is your relationship to life and business open or closed? Is your relationship loving or fearful?

- ♥ **Your customers:** Who are your customers? What are their desires? What are their fears? How is it that they relate and respond to you and others in the market?

- ♥ **Your suppliers, staff and associates:** Who are they? What are their desires and fears, and how do they relate to themselves, what they do, others and the world?

♥ **Your competitors:** Who are they? What do they fear? What do they wish and hope for? How is it that they relate and respond to these issues?

The power of relationships and cooperation

Once you realize *everything* in life is interconnected and inter-dependent, and that you are a powerful part of the whole, you will start to seek, spot and create opportunities. The richer and deeper the relationships you build are, and the stronger the glue between you and your network, customers, staff, suppliers and contacts, the greater the possibilities. In Chapter 3 you identified who inspired you and your virtual mentors. One of mine would be Nelson Mandela, who following a long struggle and imprisonment became president and rebuilt his country on cooperation and inclusiveness. It is an almost impossible story made possible only by his stopping and realizing the human condition, our co-dependence and the power of cooperation.

I have spent a lot of time on desire, fear and interrelationship because only if you truly grasp and embrace them can the magic that you wish to happen in your life, business, relationships and world emerge.

I often say that I have only one gift and that is the gift to connect to people and to help others to connect to themselves. But I realize it's a powerful gift. That connectivity is something that we all share, and it is a space that the soul trader emanates from.

I remember first realizing this in my first job. A few years in I was asked by my manager to apply for the more senior post of press officer. I was unsure I had the confidence to do it. I wasn't formally trained as a journalist. I'd simply learnt on the job from the age of 18 and progressed by building strong connections with the staff and being personable with the journalists. I realized that to get the 'ear' of busy journalists and get senior staff to cooperate I had to under-stand and charm. Working in the media – dealing with stories and campaigns – you're often dealing with an 'invisible' product rather than a tangible one, so relationships are everything. When I was asked to apply for this job I suddenly realized that I had a skill that many didn't have – the ability really to connect and develop strong relationships. At that moment a voice in my head said 'Rasheed, you have people skills – if you have people skills you can do anything.' This was the birth of the realization that actually everything is relationships and if you're able to develop rich relationships then the knowledge, support, resources and connections that you need will flow.

Likewise everything I have achieved in my entire life has been based on this one skill: in media, as a singer, as Samaritans co-director, as a coach and as a speaker. Every job I've gained, all the publications I've written for, the regular slots I've had on radio stations, becoming the business coach partner for the British Library, writing this book: they have all emerged from the power of relating and cooperating. Creating opportunities in this way does not require money, simply heart.

Rasheed's rule: Be genuinely interested in everyone you meet, and everyone you meet will be genuinely interested in you.

Relationships that last and are fruitful cannot be faked or forced. In order for somebody to be interested in you (and what you do), first you must be interested in that person. If you are *genuinely interested* in everybody you meet, everybody you meet will be genuinely interested in you. It is almost a universal truth. There will be a few exceptions of those unable or unwilling to connect, but only a few. As soon as you apply this to your business and personal life you'll find that people become powerfully drawn to you (perhaps for the first time). This is why two people doing the same job in the same business can have a similar conversation with the same customer and one will get a result and win business and the other will not. The product is the same – but the relationship is different. Countless salespeople fail because they focus on the sell and not the person. If like me you are selling an 'invisible' service then this is even more essential. Unless you connect with the *person* you do not have a hope of making a sale unless the person's relationship to your product is so strong already, which is rare if you're a small or new business. Even if it is, the relation will soon wither away if you don't truly connect.

Building your business through relationships

Where are you now? And what people, opportunities and expertise do you need?

Be clear; be specific. Revisit your notes from the previous chapters if need be. Maybe it's customers, contacts or expertise.

FIGURE 4.2   What help and cooperation do you need?

Starting out?

When I started I needed to understand business structures and tax rules and regulations. I visited the Business Link and HM Revenue and Customs websites. But I still needed someone to help me understand it all. I found a few events and workshops to help. I needed an accountant to help me understand and keep track of the financials. I asked people I knew to recommend one. I selected one who had a personable approach and was also a musician and so understood the creative side of my business. I networked with fellow coaches I trained with and joined the London Chamber of Commerce. I converted a room to coach people from and put in a new telephone line for my business. I developed filing systems. I got financial spreadsheets from my accountant. My best friend developed my first two websites and my first business card.

I didn't know it but I also needed a lawyer to help me set up terms and conditions for my business – something that many people overlook or don't realize. Fortunately, while networking, I met Helen, the lawyer turned business adviser. We swapped skills: I got terms and conditions and she got coaching sessions for her business. It worked brilliantly, cost nothing, but added extra value to us both in understanding the other's work. I needed customers, and the first few were former colleagues, friends and entertainer contacts. I was up and running – and all this through my own contacts.

If you're starting out you may need similar things. If you're producing a product, hiring staff or need premises, there will be other help needed. You may also need advice on raising finance or protecting your ideas or inventions.

Established and looking to grow?

If you're looking to grow in size, sales, customers, profit or profile you may need some similar help and support or perhaps some more specific expertise. Perhaps you need help with sales, raising or managing finance, marketing, website development, online marketing, admin support, new contacts to enter new markets, or other support.

When you've been up and running for some time it's easy to overlook just how vital and powerful cooperation is. If you have staff, are they fully informed and engaged? If you have customers, do they know all the services and products you sell? Could suppliers, contacts, friends and other people be referring business to you? Could you be helping them more? Do you actually tell people you meet what you do and what you need? Are your relationships with people rich enough that others would want to help?

Unleash your network

OK, let's find that help and support via your contacts. They say we all know around 200 people. Today with the boom in online and social media many people may have double that number of connections – often more. But in all the busyness of life we forget or overlook them or are overwhelmed – or we do not know how to make use of them.

Figure 4.3 represents the huge web of people you know. Take a large piece of paper. I am about to guide you through an exercise that will help you to:

1 list everyone you know;

2 identify everyone who may be useful;

3 identify the approach to yield the results you seek.

Using the following headings I want you to list everyone you know. This will take you some time, but it will lead you to thousands of pounds' worth of business over time. I know this, because this exercise is not just to identify and access those you know but also those whom they know. That means that the approximately 200 people whom you know can give you access potentially to 40,000 people. It's fair to say that the customers, connections and expertise can be reached in and through this pool of people. Not convinced? Then why do you think that social network websites are so powerful and have revolutionized the way that people – and businesses – connect (and sell)?

FIGURE 4.3   The web of people you know

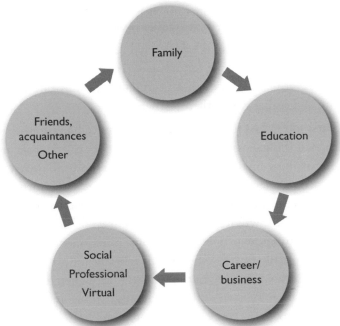

You're going to capture everyone by means of: **chronology in your life**, from those you knew first until most recently; and **category or compartment in your life**, so that you can easily identify and group them. At this stage, list everybody; don't edit people out thinking 'This person won't be useful.' Also don't worry whether you're currently in contact with someone or not. Nowadays it's easy to track people down, and we'll explore how to approach them later. Use your mobile phone, address book, database and e-mail list, and open business or social networking sites to help prompt you. The only people not to list are those you really do not like or trust:

- ♥ **Family:** List all your family members. When it comes to business many people forget that their family also have skills and connections.
- ♥ **Friends:** Likewise we often forget our friends when we think about business. Include friends of friends and acquaintances.

♥ **School, college, university:** Many of these people may love to hear from you and, again, you may not know who they know now. I recently met up with Andrew, a very good school friend who is now among the UK's most senior civil servants. I'm not going to say 'Hey, Andrew, which MPs can you introduce me to for me to coach?' after a gap of however many years, but it's certainly worth us catching up and seeing where there's synergy.

♥ **First job to last job:** List all the jobs you've had (or any previous businesses). Go through each job, role by role and department by department, and list everybody. My early coaching clients included former colleagues and a former boss. Remember, this is a marketing exercise too; many of these people will have rich networks and contacts and are bound to know people who at some point might be able to make use of your services. This is relevant for everyone – not just for those starting out in business. Very often the longer you've been in business the more ready, willing and able you may be to serve these contacts. Don't think just of the obvious managers, directors and so on. The receptionist at my first job became my landlady. Years later I was giving a talk at the Ministry of Justice and, as I walked into reception, guess who was behind the desk? Receptionists, secretaries and personal assistants are often gatekeepers and can be good door openers too.

♥ **Lost contact:** List everyone you've lost contact with: friends, contacts and customers. The beauty of this internet age is that you can probably find most of them.

♥ **Online contacts:** List all those people you haven't already listed who are social media and professional online network contacts. Log on and list them.

♥ **Customers:** List existing customers and lapsed customers. You may wish to use separate headings. Also produce a list for leads and enquiries. If you have customers, I can guarantee there are some you could call. I remember the first time I did this my customer said 'How funny you should call me. I was just thinking about...', and booked some more coaching sessions.

♥ **Social, sports and voluntary organizations:** Are you or have you been a member of any? If so, list all the names. This can be a powerful way of spreading the word among their individual and collective networks.

♥ **Ambassadors and fans:** This is a very important category. List everybody who really likes, respects and trusts you. These people love you and what you do. They'll go the extra mile to help you. They sing your praises at every opportunity and will tell everyone how great you are. These are a key group that you tell what you're doing and what you're looking for – these people will connect you to those who can help you. Often they will go out of their way to put you in touch with contacts, potential customers and so forth, but in order to do this effectively they need to know what you want and need.

♥ **Ace networkers:** This is another important group. Who are the people you know who are really well connected and seem to know everybody? There may well be a crossover with other lists, as these people often fall into a few categories for the very reason that they are ace networkers.

♥ **Other business owners and professionals:** List all the other business owners (or managers within them) whom you know. If you are already in business you may want to produce a few separate lists under the relevant subheadings that relate to what you do or what you need.

♥ **Suppliers:** List all the suppliers you have and do work with. This may include equipment suppliers, printers, trainers, consultants, events organizers and all sorts of other companies and specialists. These people may prove very useful to you and your other contacts and customers.

♥ **Others:** Add any other headings and names that may be useful for you. For example, if you run an online business or want access to some you might list 'Online business contacts' as a heading.

I remember doing a version of this exercise with a group of business owners. One of the attendees was a landscape gardener. He was looking for some more wealthy clients with bigger gardens, which would mean that he'd be able to grow his profits. I asked 'Who do you *already* know who has money?' Lo and behold, he knew two people who fitted the bill. You may think 'Surely he would have asked them.' In my experience most business owners have 'blind spots' about who they know and do not 'mine' their network as deeply as they could or are too shy to ask.

The art of utilizing your network

Now you have a list of all sorts of people from all the areas and stages of your life. You may already have all sorts of thoughts and ideas about who to contact. You may also be wondering about how to contact them or what to say without coming across as desperate, pushy or presumptuous.

1 **Tick the names of everyone who may be useful.** The different people you know will be useful in differing ways. Some may be potential clients. Some may have excellent contacts in areas you want to access. Some people may have skills that can help you: building websites, sales and marketing. Others may simply have lots of contacts or experience. Tick their names and write a short phrase to indicate the way in which they may be useful. For example, you might indicate: 'help with my website'; 'may know good accountant'; 'potential client'; 'access to corporate contact'; 'knows people who may finance my business'; 'runs own business'; 'may know good salespeople' – and so on.

2 **What's the win–win, or what's the angle?** Many people fail to utilize their network and contacts because they are selfish, greedy, insensitive, fearful or short-sighted. The soul trader is mindful of reciprocal relationships. So what is the win–win? Consider each person in turn. How can you help the person? Where is the person at in life and in business? In some cases you may know or be able to find out or ask. Maybe you have contacts who may be useful for someone. Friends, fans

and ambassadors on your list are likely to help you because the relationship is already strong and because they really want to help you. Even so, be mindful of how you and others in your network might help them now or later. Your skill with IT, websites, healing treatments or whatever you do may be a lovely thank-you and help to them. This is not about bribing. Never use it as such. It is about exchanging skills and helping them in a way that is helpful to *them*.

3 **How and when to approach people.** I love this part. What's the best way to approach each person on your list? Everyone is an individual, and all have their own personalities, preferences and circumstances. Think about it from their perspective, not yours – just as we did in Chapter 2 ('Customers'). What medium works well for them: phone, e-mail, social networking site, lunch, coffee, letter, text message? There's no point e-mailing someone just because it suits you if the person rarely opens e-mail and prefers connecting on social networking sites.

TIP Consider people's style. Are they businesslike, and do they prefer people to get straight to the point? Do they like to catch up socially over coffee? With extremely busy people it's often wiser to ask for 10 minutes than an hour (that way they'll probably say yes and will give you more time). We will pick up and build on this in Chapter 5 ('Conversations'). Thoughtfulness and consideration are vital. Some people's entire business and marketing strategy is based purely on this insight and approach.

TIP Good timing is everything. Be aware of what stage you are at and how ready your product or service is in relation to the advice or outcome that you may seek. If you're making contact for research, help and advice, then an early-stage contact may be good (depending on the help and advice you seek). If it is about being introduced to potential contacts and customers then in most cases you need to ensure that you and your product are good and ready.

Building a winning team on a shoestring budget

Simon is a singer who has adopted this cooperative approach. He hired me as a coach for his mindset and also hired a vocal coach. He was proactive, learnt about the industry and spent lots of time networking, through which he found the right producer and manager, who trusted his values. Through these relationships he gained new contacts, gigs and shows. He worked part time to support himself. Some of the support he hired; other support he was able to get to help him out just by the sheer (quiet) force of his personality and his genuine commitment to what he was doing. It paid off: in 2010 he supported Whitney Houston on her tour of Europe!

Advancing with your ambassadors

Heather is one of my most valued business contacts. Her business helps businesses manage their finances and operations from bookkeeping to advice on selling the business. Heather and I cooperate, swapping sessions periodically. At one such meeting she said 'Almost all my clients come to me by word of mouth and my existing clients and contacts.' She'd identified the key ambassadors and we came up with a powerful way of thanking them and helping them to recommend her. She realized that while they knew about some aspects of her services they didn't know about others, so she sent them a personalized stationery holder for their desks – to keep her business in their minds – and a travel card holder that contained two business cards for Heather's business (so that they could pass one on). The business card was designed in the style of a tube or subway map, but instead of station names the list was of all Heather's company's services to prompt her 'ambassadors' with all the services she could provide. It's an effective strategy. The stationery holder is on my desk, and I use the travel card holder daily. These handy gifts inform her ambassadors and keep her business in their minds, so referring business to her is easy. How can you help your ambassadors refer business to you?

Personable, professional, delivering

You now have several leads and contacts, but it's essential you get the right support for you and your business. I apply the three rules shown in Table 4.2 for those I choose to work with.

TABLE 4.2 Personable, professional, delivering

> 1. *Personable:* Are they likeable, warm and personable? Do you like and get on with them and respect them as human beings? Do they have the ability and sensibility genuinely to treat each individual as such? If they do not have this quality, why would you want to work with them, and can they actually serve your customers?
>
>
>
> 2. *Professional:* Are they qualified to do the job that you wish them to do and that they say they can do? Do they carry out their work to a high professional standard? Do they have the reputation and presentation and conduct themselves well in line with those standards?
>
>
>
> 3. *Delivering:* Do they do what they do, when they say they will do it, to the standard they say that they will?

If they tick all three boxes then you are in a very good place. I recommend that everyone in your business network, and those you add to it, tick all three boxes. There may be occasional tasks where someone may not have or need a professional paper qualification. Nonetheless they need to be able to do a professional job, and it's worth you being mindful of all three boxes being ticked. As far as I am concerned all these boxes need to be ticked in order for all concerned to flourish. If the contacts are not personable then the business relationship will break down sooner or later. If they are not professional then you're asking for trouble and may well get it; and you and your customers may suffer, and your reputation may be damaged for ever. If people cannot or do not deliver to a certain standard – which should be high – then any or all of the issues outlined may befall you, your business and your customers. This means you too must also be personable and professional and must deliver. You may well need to go and work on your skills, your service and your product.

The beauty of being your own boss is that there are many ways in which you can build your business through relationships, from informally getting friends, family and contacts to help you through to hiring staff and bringing on board formal business partners. Some of them are highlighted in Figure 4.4. It depends on what suits you and the size, scale and saleability of your business. For many a soul trader the type of support and collaboration sought works organically if you go clockwise around the diagram in Figure 4.4.

FIGURE 4.4   Support and collaboration

♥ **Ad hoc services/virtual support:** There will be times when you buy in expertise as and when you need it: graphic designers, photographers, relevant suppliers and so on. I also add virtual support here, as some people hire in virtual assistants on a project, pay-as-you-go or ongoing basis to support them.

♥ **Network and customers:** We've already touched on how you could use your existing network to generate opportunities, and in a moment we'll stop and take a look at building it through networking, including utilizing membership organizations. My clients and event attendees regularly tell me that 90 per cent of their business comes from these combined sources. This is 'word-of-mouth power'.

♥ **Barter/swapping and cross-promoting:** Strangely, given that we started off as a species bartering and exchanging, this is underused. It is powerful if it is done from a place of real mutual benefit.

♥ **Associates:** Very often developing strong contacts with others in our own field or related or complementary fields can lead to all sorts of opportunities. Associate relationships can work in all sorts of ways, from two trainers teaming up to deliver a joint promotional workshop and perhaps splitting the costs and profits, to something on a more long-term basis of working together that may involve referral fees or incentives. Who in your network could you be teaming up with or working alongside on projects?

♥ **Joint ventures and formal partnerships:** These often emerge naturally where you've already worked informally as associates. This may take many forms, from your realizing you want to bring another expert into your business (and/or the person's money, resources and contacts) to other collaborative arrangements.

♥ **Paid staff:** You may have gone full circle from paying for one-off or occasional support to where you need to hire staff on a full- or part-time basis. It involves formality, rules, regulations, costs and consideration but can also takes things to a whole new level.

The first three can work very well and smoothly with little or no formality. The final three – starting with more complex or involved associate arrangements through to hiring staff – will require agreements, contracts and the correct legal advice and structure.

All this points to the value of developing a rich and diverse network of contacts and expertise so that, as your business, aspirations and customers' needs develop, you have the support and contacts to grow with it.

Let's take a close look at some of the ways in which networking may work for you.

From not working to effective networking

Many people hate networking events, find them tedious and feel they are ineffective. In most cases that's because they do not know what networking is, assume that they have some divine right to gain business, and do not know how to connect with people.

- ♥ **Myth and failure:** Networking is not about going out, telling everyone what you do, giving them your business card and hoping and assuming they will get in touch and give you business. Remember, nobody cares about you or what you do yet.

- ♥ **Reality and success:** Networking is about having conversations, learning and making connections that may be mutually beneficial. The secret again is taking a genuine interest in the other person and finding out about what the person does. You're on the lookout for personable professionals who deliver. If someone does not ask you about you then that person has failed already. To network effectively and win business from it you need to communicate clearly, concisely, effectively and flexibly. We'll pick up on how you can have conversations that generate real opportunities in the next chapter. A blend of networking in person and online often works best.

Where should I network?

1 **Network where potential customers are:** Chat, find out and take an interest. What kind of events do your potential customers attend? Research, find out and ask others whom you know, like and trust.

2 **Network where your peers and suppliers are:** Make contacts and spot opportunities. Attend events that your peers, suppliers and competitors are at. This may include industry events, conferences and exhibitions, trade association networking evenings, launches and so on. Research, join relevant mailing lists and attend. Many of these events are great for learning about new developments, making contact with 'the great and the good' and meeting other like-minded people, including potential contacts and associates.

3 **Network where key industry figures are:** Become visible, respected and in touch. There's often a large crossover with point 2 above. Very often key industry figures address conferences and shows, but you may also find that they address business organizations or other events in your industry. Publications, newsletters or websites related to your field may be useful. These events can be good for becoming informed, asking shrewd questions that get you noticed and making useful contacts.

4 **Business and industry organizations** – and others in your sector and related sectors – are great resources. Many also provide a range of networking and business development services, including legal support or business advice as part of the membership. Look out for like-minded potential associates who provide either the same or complementary services. In fact look out for great people of all professions,

as you never know what help you or those in your network may need. Strong friendships and peer support are developed this way. Connect with competitors too; you can learn, and you may find scope to work together, build capacity and refer business in a way that raises everyone's game – as athletes do.

5 **Chance, social life and 'non'-networking:** When you run a business every situation is a possible situation to make contacts. It may not always be appropriate, and you may be 'off duty', but like a medic always be ready. I have made good contacts when I've been in a café. Being armed with business cards for those train journeys, trips, parties, visits to the gym or volunteers' meetings can be useful.

The blend of networking

Karen the recruitment specialist did the exercise of listing her contacts that you've done and identified about 10–15 good contacts from her own network to follow up on, many of which are likely to lead to work now or in the future. We also identified two or three memberships and groups for her to join and get involved in, which may also lead to contacts and opportunities. This blend will ensure that Karen is in touch with customers, useful contacts and key players in her industry. In time it will bring in more income and more opportunities.

Seven steps to great relationships

1 **Rapport** – a warm, genuine connection; open and friendly, not heavy or pushy.

2 **Respect** – learn about each other's skills, style, strengths and specialisms.

3 **Relationship** – if there is synergy and likeability a connection naturally occurs.

4 **Reliability and responsibility** – diligence and delivering are how trust grows.

5 **Relay and refer** – sharing information, skills, support, contacts, ideas and work.

6 **Result** – business, customers, joint initiatives and happy customers emerge.

7 **Reciprocate (throughout)** – a two-way, mutual, 'win–win' approach throughout.

Swapping skills, sampling and sharing

I've touched on the fact that I had few resources and not much money when I started. I also knew very little about business or where to go. I went to a number of general networking events and some specifically in and around my industry. At one of those events I met Helen, a former lawyer, and Heather the business finance specialist. Helen and Heather also knew Suzanne, who produced websites and design, and Helen and I had met Nicole, who was a marketing specialist. We realized that we had similar clients, similar values and a similar personable and professional style. We realized that we could refer business and clients to one another sure in the knowledge that they'd get a great service. We also swapped our own coaching, legal, marketing and web design services among ourselves, which meant that we got not only free support that would have cost us thousands of pounds, but also an understanding of each other's work and business so that we could become ambassadors and advocates of each other's business.

Collaboration and complementary businesses

Exchanging skills led the group of us to form Zestworks, an umbrella site through which we showcased and cross-referred work. It brought us more work and gave us a louder voice and clout. Not only did we cross-refer business but we ran a few events and wrote a book – easy when you pool resources.

Who could you collaborate with? Perhaps you're a lawyer and could be cross-referring more work to solicitors or to accountants and other professional services. Lots of this goes on formally and informally.

This is a way of working Donald the surveyor is keen to introduce. He already wins some business through this method, but has now identified a number of providers of legal and estate agent services in his area and is building relationships with them to refer business.

Team power

A few years ago I decided to make a pilot TV show: *The Rasheed Show: Be the Change, See the Change.* I'd been approached by TV companies to present shows, but I'd never been chosen. I realized I'd need camera operators, a studio, a website, an editor, a set designer, promotion, people to interview and possibly other support too. I tapped into my network. The result was a fairly good pilot that boosted my TV portfolio and profile that might have cost around £10,000 to make, but was made for a fraction of that cost by pooling our talents.

Skills exchange and free samples

Do you offer a free taster so others can experience, enjoy, buy or recommend the product? The 'test drive' has been used in the car industry for decades, and you'd think it absurd if a shop didn't let you try on clothes first. Carefully consider it so that your potential customer or referrer really values it. Be mindful of your time, resources and investment and the possible returns. Ambassadors, suppliers, introducers and high-value repeat customers are certainly worth doing this for. The key words here are 'complimentary, not free' – 'complimentary' suggests you're giving a gift or covering the charge; 'free' suggests it has no costs.

Entrepreneurs have differing views on this, and some (often premium products) deliberately do not. Perhaps give tasters on selected products. Be clear on your policy so you can justify it to yourself (and others if challenged). This is not about coercing or favouring people; it's about giving people a chance to experience it. This works well as part of a focused pricing, discounting and concession strategy. See what others do across industries and what might work for you.

I estimate that I have received £250,000 worth of help, support and services by exchanging, sharing and swapping skills with all sorts of professionals, and I have used it as part of my overall promotional, customer and contacts strategy.

Advance with associates

The beauty of associates is that you can work with similar or complementary specialists or businesses, bringing more skill, style and expertise to your business.

Zestworks was a good example; you may know many more. Many big companies do this effectively too through cross-promotion. Because you're still separate entities and manage your own company or have self-employment status, the practicalities typically concern simply working out the services to deliver jointly and who leads on a particular project and sorting out the fees and financials that usually go through the relevant associates' business.

Nadine is an accomplished finance and business TV presenter, chairs international conferences, and runs a presentation skills business. We met through a networking event through Neville, a mutual contact, and instantly started chatting about our shared media backgrounds. As serendipity would have it, one of her clients – Associated Press, the largest news agency in the world – was building additional TV studios in central London, and Nadine was working in partnership with it to offer TV media training programmes. She needed an experienced TV presenter and found one. It was a timely win–win for us both. This kind of serendipity of finding good associates becomes common for soul traders, who are always looking for great people.

Nadine says:

> *I've always worked with associates because it works for me, my business, my lifestyle and my clients. My work takes me across the world, and I need help from a variety of people with a range of expertise for all the different projects, so having fixed offices or a big staff team has not been necessary; working with associates is economical and gives flexibility. The challenge is getting it right. One of the things I have done though – and Rasheed's prompting has helped me – is to introduce one core member of staff to work on sales and business development, and I wish I had made that appointment years ago. I'm a working mum to two children, and I could not run my business without support. I have family and people I love and trust who help with childcare as and when, and I'm lucky to work with a team. The key is having excellent associates with current and relevant experience – otherwise it wouldn't work.*

Motoring with mentoring

A very powerful way to raise one's game is through mentoring. Mentoring is essentially where someone who has 'been there and done it' mentors someone who is on the way. It goes on all the time informally. You may be a mentor or mentee without naming or knowing it. The learning, contacts, and scope to avoid the pitfalls and fast-track can be immense. Who could mentor you? Who could you mentor? The key is that the personalities and expectations match. I know many accomplished people who have various mentors and coaches to help them at each new stage of their growth.

There are also some formal mentoring organizations and groups in various sectors where mentoring may take place formally or informally. It can be very powerful, especially if you are entering a new industry.

David is an experienced sales professional setting up a new car parts business. He had built a successful business before and realized that he wanted mentoring for his new business for the specific expertise and guidance, and because he realized that he works best when he has someone else to help motivate, challenge and support. He joined TiE, which is a mentoring organization that has chapters across the world.

David is in fact using the whole blend of approaches we've covered in this chapter, as his business will need to find finance, relationships with stockists, a factory and staff. He accessed his network, gained the support of a former colleague who is an experienced former operations manager, and has a very good industry contact who is interested in his product. During our sessions he also identified that he wants a business partner (as he had in the past), so right now he's exploring who from his contacts and those he is meeting might fit the bill.

The boost of a business partner

Robert runs an IT software business. When we met he was making a lot of money but working incredibly hard. He was keen to move from being largely a one-person business to building a sustainable business. What impressed me was his remarkable drive and that he realized the power of bringing in other exceptional people to help him. He consulted various experts and took me on as coach to help him stay on track, but one of his most inspired moves was a simple and profound one. At one of my networking events he met Neville, a semi-retired, highly active, accomplished marketing expert with senior-level contacts in many industries. They talked, developed a strong rapport and looked at how they could help each other. Robert brought Neville on board initially on a part-time basis and paid him well. Through Neville, Robert gained access to major corporate clients. Two years on, they have a team of around eight, a client list that includes major banks, and international contacts in the offing. In less than two years Robert has taken himself from being essentially a single-person business to the owner of a niche business with an impressive contact list and huge growth prospects from overseas.

Bringing in or starting out with business partners raises many questions that you need to consider, including:

♥ What exactly do you want to achieve?

♥ What type and level of help and involvement do you want in your business?

♥ Do you want an active business partner or partners or someone to support you financially or with expertise?

♥ What are your individual goals within and beyond business, and how do they dovetail?

♥ Do you like, trust and respect this person/these people?

♥ How well do you know this person/these people – and yourself?

♥ How will the arrangement work financially, managerially and operationally? Be specific.

♥ What level of risk do you feel comfortable with?

♥ How strong or open is the communication that you have and that will be required?

♥ What is your starting growth strategy and your exit strategy?

♥ What is the track reputation and record of all concerned?

♥ Can you work with this person?

♥ How do you all cope under pressure? What if things go wrong?

♥ What agreements and arrangements need to be put in place?

Ensure that you have all the answers; the process of working together with any potential partners may itself be telling.

The shrewd entrepreneur will do the right talking, courting and getting to know and trust before committing. Perhaps working on a few projects together may help you identify if you can and should work together. Getting advice and ensuring that the right agreements are in place are very important. This is where a strong and rich network of contacts may serve you well. There may be those who have walked this path who can help, guide and advise you, and you may be able to consult the right legal and financial expertise in your network. However, you are the one who will have to 'live with' and work with the person. The practical considerations are not the only ones; ensure that you are happy with the arrangement emotionally, ethically and spiritually. If it does not feel right then it is unlikely to work. As with all relationships, the issue is not so much how you feel when all is rosy and going well but whether you could work it out, fix it and build on it if the road got rocky or times got tough.

Hiring and inspiring staff

Perhaps like Robert you're on a business growth path. You may have staff or be thinking about it. In my experience taking on that first staff member is the biggest practical and emotional challenge that soul traders have. Mirtha is an independent human resources specialist who set up her own consultancy to help small businesses with hiring staff after 20 years of heading HR within large organizations. We met through networking, spotted the synergy and value we could add to each other's business clients and also joined the Zestworks team. Mirtha says:

> When a sole trader finds the need to move on to the next stage, ie to get additional support, there are a number of factors to take into consideration, ranging from getting casual help, use of freelancers, employing staff, etc. It is very important to get your employment practices right from the start in a way that works for you, for your employees and in the eyes of the law. Employment law is very complex, and compliance is compulsory for all employers large and small. Changes to rules and regulations do occur with a certain frequency, which makes it very difficult for small employers to keep up to date.

Mirtha's top 10 tips

1 Assess the type of requirement, ie regular work, seasonal or project based.

2 The answer to point 1 above will help you decide if you need a seasonal person or the use of a freelancer as and when demand increases.

3 If you opt for a freelancer, ensure that you put in place a formal agreement signed by both parties so that the business relationship is clear from the start and your business is protected.

4 If you opt for an employee, before starting your recruitment process clearly define what the tasks of the employee will be, what you are prepared to delegate, and what qualifications and experience you require to meet your business needs. This is done through what is called a job description and a job specification.

5 Prepare questions for the interview in advance to ensure that you are consistent in your selection process.

6 Avoid questions that could lead to claims of discrimination, such as those related to age, disability or gender.

7 Once you appoint your employee ensure that you issue a contract of employment within the first eight weeks of employment.

8 Do take up references and implement a probationary period review to assess suitability.

9 Maintain a good communication and feedback system, carry out regular appraisals and capture and resolve minor issues before they become unmanageable.

10 If you need to discipline the employee or terminate employment, make sure you do so fairly and in compliance with relevant regulations.

Mirtha adds: 'Communication and cooperation are key throughout the employment cycle. I sadly continue to see organizations big and small that due to failing to communicate and give feedback on a regular basis allow simple situations to get out of hand, which invariably leads to conflict and the expensive resolution of broken employment relationships.'

Here are my tips to keep your staff inspired once they're in place:

1 **Destination:** All must know and be on board with vision, mission and progress.

2 **Designation:** Ensure everyone is clear about their and others' roles.

3 **Regulations:** Ensure staff know those that relate and apply to them.

4 **Delegation:** Ensure that you pass tasks down, up and across appropriately.

5 **Communication:** Make sure this is in all directions to keep the team and customers happy.

6 **Dedication:** Ensure that everyone is engaged, effective and supported.

7 **Appreciation:** Give praise and feedback and help everyone to grow and develop.

Cooperative team spirit

This collaborative approach is something that Parit, the founder of Jutebag.co.uk, has introduced. Parit is a classic 'soul trader', who with his business partner based the business on ethical, environmental and ecological principles. Their bags are reusable and made of jute, a natural fibre. When we met they were already doing well supplying to major companies, charities and retailers. They were a company also acting cooperatively supporting schools in the area of India where the jute was sourced. Now looking to expand from the UK into Europe, Parit gained the finance through 'crowd funding' from like-minded entrepreneurs.

Parit wanted a collaborative spirit in his organization, so he's introducing a scheme to give staff benefits, opportunities to develop their skills, team bonding and social events. In the longer term he plans to give employees shares in the company. Parit also recognized the need for a new, more visionary approach to keep his growing team on track and inspired, while still keeping his friendly style. Parit puts it plainly: 'Cooperation is a very powerful tool within and outside business. It is basically a two-way traffic lane; if you are helpful, caring and understanding you get that back.'

Get it right; seek help and advice

So cooperation can fast-track you and your business, but still many business owners drown by not calling out for help when they need it. Don't be one of them.

Simple things

Sometimes getting help with small things can have a major impact. For years I painstakingly booked people personally on to my workshops. It was silly. It took up huge amounts of time. I also knew I could set up an electronic payment system – but it wasn't my strength. Eventually I asked Suzanne, who masterminds my website, if she could do it. She set up the page and the branding and linked it to my website in 30 minutes!

Significant things

When I set up a retreats company with my yoga teacher friend Thierry it required liaising with my accountant, legal adviser and web designer. It required working with venue finders, venues, airlines and retreat centres. Most of all it required a huge amount of cooperation – and dare I even say compromise – between us. This can be a huge step: from making all the decisions to consulting someone else regarding key decisions. We had to decide on roles and responsibilities. It was often difficult, but the learning curve was invaluable. At such times having a skilled network is invaluable.

While it's important to get things right and to get the right professional advice, there will be times where you do not get it right. This takes us back to my personable, professional and delivering mantra. If things go wrong when you are working with such people, the situation is invariably salvageable and you'll learn and grow. A year into the retreats business we realized that it wasn't working well and that it would be simpler to run future events via our separate companies. Had we not been friends and respected each other professionally this might have had deeply damaging effects on our business and our friendship. As it happened our customers got a great service – again down to the approach of putting people and relationships first.

SUMMARY

The secret of cooperation and collaboration is finding the right style and blend for you. The art is that over time you develop a rich personal and professional network that can help you with any issue that may arise for you and your business. Whether the expertise is employed, hired as necessary or exchanged for mutual benefit is dependent on you and your business and its stage. This approach can benefit everyone: you, your customers and the wider needs of those in and around your network.

Top tips are:

1 **Strategic:** Carefully consider the contacts and opportunities you want and ensure that everyone on board is skilled and motivated, and knows where you're heading and the path you're taking.

2 **Natural and organic:** Collaborations work when there is a natural conception, birth, growth, maturing and passing. Don't force it; nurture it – and know when to bring it to a close.

3 **Operational:** Put the right support, structures, systems and staff in place. How will it be managed, delivered, developed, promoted, reviewed and improved?

4 **Financial:** Collaborations are an investment that should pay off financially – directly or indirectly. Stay mindful of costs and cash flow.

5 **Legal:** Get it right and get advice, or it could end in tears, tatters, tantrums and trouble.

6 **Equitable:** It must be a win–win situation where everyone benefits. If not, it will be a stressful and unhappy journey.

7 **Personable, professional and delivering:** As with all relationships, love, trust and respect are the key – and maintain high standards and ethics.

CONVERSATIONS

How to convert contacts into customers

Open sesame: The right word said at the right time will unlock a door to unknown treasures. The wrong word will close them up to you for ever.

We express life through language and connect through conversations. They go on every minute of every day and affect every aspect of our personal and business lives. The problem is that so often they are not:

♥ **relevant and timely enough** – for one or all parties really to listen or engage;

♥ **interesting enough** – for one or all parties to pay appropriate attention to and pursue;

♥ **simple and straightforward enough** – to understand and remember;

♥ **loud or gentle enough** – to us to be able to hear or wish to hear;

♥ **sweet or savoury enough** – to really appeal to us;

♥ **compelling enough** – for one or more parties to act on.

As we've discovered, almost everyone you meet is a potential customer or connector – but in the whirlwind of business marketing and living life is yours just one voice in the blizzard?

Everything you do and say in business is a conversation – or potential conversation:

♥ What are you saying (verbally and non-verbally) when and if you meet people?

♥ What is your website and business card promotional material saying?

♥ What are your social media saying and communicating?

♥ What are others in your life and industry saying?

♥ What are other people saying about you?

♥ What is it that those you are meeting actually want to talk about?

Customer conversion is dependent on the right customer conversation.

You are now at the point in this book – in your journey – where it all boils down to winning customers and opportunities.

It is all about **customer conversion,** and this ultimately depends on the right **customer conversation.** If you like:

Right product + Right time + Right conversation = Sale

All of these factors are important. First, your product needs to be right for your customer. That is your job. This book will help, and it's also the result of your ongoing relationship and dialogue with your customers. Once you have a good product and systems – and are talking to enough of the right people – your success will depend on how relevant your message, your conversations and your communication are.

♥ Are you telling (enough of the right) people about what you do?

♥ Are you having two-way, rich, genuine dialogues that are win–win?

♥ Are you having the right conversations with those who could help you?

♥ Are all your materials really speaking to those you wish to serve?

Sadly this is where so many businesses fall down. Our conversations at networking events are dull and unmemorable. Our letters and e-mails are long and rambling. The wording on our websites is gobbledegook. Worse still, we don't tell people what we are doing – or we speak and present our products without passion. If you're not passionate about your products, why should anyone else be? If you don't tell those close to you what you're doing, how do you expect those further afield to hear about it?

Very often, the conversations alone separate those who succeed and those who do not. The beauty of conversations is that, when combined with the cooperation approach, they do not cost (or do not cost a lot). On the other hand, getting the conversations wrong or not having them at all can be very costly.

In this chapter we will explore among other things:

♥ the psychology of conversations and communication;

♥ the conversations that you should be having;

♥ the power of the right conversation;

♥ the best means and modes of communication for you;

♥ tips for converting those conversations into business.

I stress that this chapter is not about theory. Act on it. Put it into place from today. I want you to see it creating real opportunities in your life and in your business, as it has in mine.

The psychology

This is a five-minute guide to how to understand and influence everyone you meet. The problem with most conversations – as we've seen – is that most are about 'me, me, me': our view from our standpoint. However, to understand and influence people and win sales you need to understand the world of the person you're dealing with.

FIGURE 5.1   Seeing the world from our own viewpoint

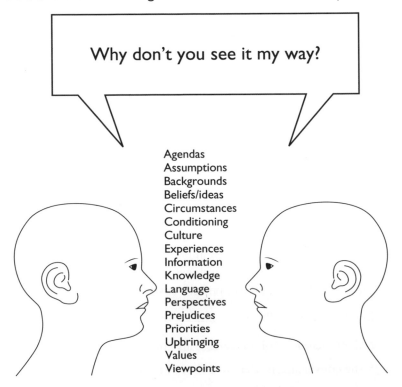

There are a whole series of factors that prevent others seeing the world the way you do. That means that at first they are deaf to what you're saying. They are in their own world, with their own agendas.

Nobody is more so than the entrepreneur. As an entrepreneur you have your product, service or cause that you keep drumming on about. But, as we've discovered, your customer, contacts, even your family, friends, lover, children or mother may not care or understand – because they're in their own world. They see it through their lens. If you like, the factors in Figure 5.1 combine to create slightly – or very – different-shaded contact lenses through which people see the world.

We share the same physical planet but live in our own worlds.

So your conversation needs to be about *their* world. Don't make assumptions about it: be open, listen and ask questions – this creates understanding and demonstrates that we're interested in them and their world.

Building rapport, relationships and influence

FIGURE 5.2   Seeing the world from the other's viewpoint

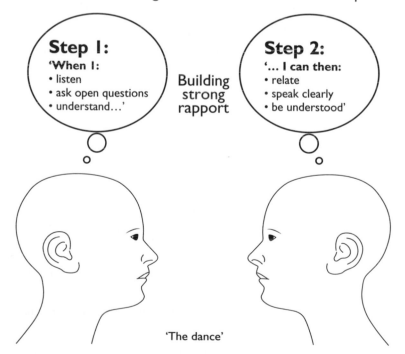

The magic happens once we change our approach and 'get out of our heads'. It happens the moment that we see the world from the other's viewpoint.

Take the classic example of going to a networking event. When networking is done badly you go up to someone, hand out your card and start spouting off about what you do and vice versa. But no rapport has taken place; you're both in your own worlds. What's more, the environment of the 'business event' means that you feel you have to act in some overly official way that bypasses the foundations of real human connectivity. This is why you leave so many events and meetings cold, remembering few people and uninspired.

The key to really building rapport and relationships is that you take an interest in the individual and in *that person's* world. If this is achieved then other possibilities may emerge. What actually happens in this slight shift is that you both move out of your own worlds into a new space that you are exploring together. This is 'the dance'. It happens very naturally when people meet like minds socially and it is how friendships are formed. It is absolutely essential in forging the kind of relationships where you can generate business purely from the power of conversations and cooperation.

So now that we've looked at the psychology we can look at building your business through rich conversations.

Are you even having conversations at all?

The first question is: are you having conversations at all? Are you connecting with contacts, your network and those you meet?

At the start of one of my networking events I got all 100 attendees on their feet and asked them to introduce themselves briefly to as many others as they could in five minutes. One was a young man who had recently started up a cleaning business. He was clearly a little shy, and after meeting just one person he retreated to his chair.

Here was this likeable guy in a safe environment of 99 other business owners, all of whom might know people who could make use of his services. He had no competitors – his was the only cleaning business there. His shyness, combined with not realizing that conversations are what winning business is all about, was crippling. Are you killing off your business by not networking and not having conversations?

This does not happen just to new businesses. I remember meeting a very successful accountant in the entertainment industry. Each new client brought in is worth many thousands of pounds to the profitability of the firm. He was extremely personable and professional. I liked him straight away, and I knew I'd recommend relevant clients of mine to him. He told me he shied away from networking. He received lots of event invitations – to good events with good-calibre leads – but he attended few. I tell you that this guy could earn many more thousands for the business if he were to go out and accept more of the invitations. I was keen to coach and help him, as I knew his warmth and personality would easily win business through conversations. As a soul trader be in the world – put your heart out there.

- ♥ Who should you be chatting to?
- ♥ What events should you be attending?
- ♥ What contacts, customers and suppliers should you be talking to?

Building your business through conversations

Here are some of the key ingredients to conversations that yield results:

1 **Aim for the right timing** (which you may not always be aware of).

2 **Be visible and be noticed** (as a business owner this is your job).

3 Be open (don't be too fixed, keep your eyes open, and trust your instincts).

4 Spot synergies and opportunities (those who fare best have this awareness).

5 Remember it's all about them (it should be appropriate to and benefit the other).

6 Have good intentions (if the energy behind it is wrong it's apt to go wrong).

7 Aim for win–win (for a conversation to convert all must stand to gain – it sparks action).

In my case an informal conversation with an associate led me to attend a British Library Inspiring Entrepreneurs event. During the panel discussion I raised a relevant and informed question, and said that I was a life and business coach. I followed up with a conversation with one of the British Library team during the networking afterward. I was visible and proactive and spotted synergy. It so happened that at that time the Library's Business and Intellectual Property Centre was developing a programme of workshops to support the services in the Centre – it was good timing. The result was that I became the partner life and business coach to the Centre, which has added to my profile, visibility and reputation as a leading business coach.

Being open is a key requirement. There is an interesting relationship between being strategic and aware of want you want to do and achieve – as we explored in Chapter 1 ('Clarity') – and being open. This blend of intention and openness is where possibility really resides. When intention (being you and doing what you do) and openness (to other people and the world) meet, magic happens.

This book also emerged as a result of meeting the Editor-at-Large of Kogan Page at a British Library event where I was speaking, which was followed by a conversation at which I was asked if I was planning to write a business book – I replied yes and followed up with an e-mail and one-page outline. The soul trader is always open to opportunities and alert to them and follows up.

In all of these cases the opportunities emerged naturally and organically, but they only did so by my understanding the world of who I was speaking to. It is a dance between you and the other party, and your objectives must align. I can't think of a single piece of business I've gained that did not come directly or indirectly from a conversation.

Conversations that get results

Here are some of the factors that will help you create opportunities from conversations. Check that you have these things in place:

- ♥ **Something to say:** You must be clear, compelling and relevant. You need a clear message of who you are, what you do and how your product helps.

- ♥ **Something to show:** Have samples or examples of your work or product, testimonials and your track record. Your track record includes what you did prior to what you're doing now. I also leverage my media and music to attract some of my speaking and coaching work.

- ♥ **Something to sample or share:** Have a way of allowing people to taste, test or test-drive your product. Can you give them a free sample or a complimentary session or place on your event?

- ♥ **Something to serve:** Ultimately your product must be of clear, direct value – of service to the people you are speaking to or those they will be introducing you to.

So let's take a look at some of the key components of what makes a conversation convert into business:

- ♥ **Objective/open:** First things first: why are you having this conversation? What *specifically* do you want to get out of it? An introduction, a piece of business, advice, something else? You need to be clear on what you want from the conversation and what action you want to unfold from it. However, in some other cases the conversation is about

FIGURE 5.3   What makes a conversation convert into business

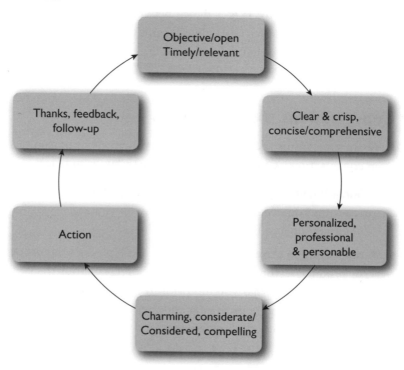

being open, exploring, learning, connecting, brainstorming or gaining or sharing advice or ideas.

♥ **Clear and crisp, concise and comprehensive:** Ensure everything that you say is clear and simple. How many events have you attended where people speak jargon or ramble? Ditch it. Know what the point is and get to it. Where you or others are busy, keep conversations short and sweet, but know when to be detailed and thorough. Sometimes you will need to combine the two.

♥ **Personalized, professional and personable:** Focus on the specific person you are speaking to and that person's business. Tailor and personalize the conversation to that individual *and* the person's business and values. This means that you may be working on two levels at the same time: the specific individual and the business in general – be aware of both sensitivities and styles. Ensure your conversations are always professional and conducted professionally. Build a reputation of being someone who delivers an excellent product, and carry yourself in the same fashion – irrespective of others' standards. Everyone in your team or representing you must also meet the same standards. Be yourself, and allow others to be themselves. This all creates a dance of you becoming liked and trusted. It is your job to ensure your approach and service mould to your customer. Being a soul trader is like running a fantastic hotel; make everyone feel as though he or she is the most important person in the world.

♥ **Charming, considerate, considered and compelling:** Charm and likeability make people want to 'buy in' and recommend you. It's the blend of warmth and 'personability' that enchants and impresses. Give others attention and importance – adding a dash of fun that can break the ice and create a powerful bond. Show consideration. Be mindful of the other person. Is it a good time to call? Would it be better to resume the meeting another time? Could you tweak the joint venture so it serves the other person's needs even more? Be thoughtful and measured. Don't make promises you can't keep. Make your conversation compelling: be interested, interesting and engaging. Be passionate about what you do, why you do it, who you help and what the benefits are. If you are passionate and focused on the person you are speaking to, you will be compelling.

♥ **Action:** So you're at the end of the meeting or the phone call, and you've exchanged details – now what? Be clear on the next steps; discuss, clarify, check everyone is happy and modify if need be. What will be done, when and by whom? The onus is on both parties to act, but ultimately you're running your business, and building it is down to you. I'm not saying that you should do all the work. I am saying the more proactive you are the more you will steer the ship. This is a subtle point; never force or push, but be aware of what plates are spinning and which need to be set in motion.

♥ **Thanks, feedback and follow-up:** 'Thanks' is a short, powerful word with a long aftershock. Whether it's a follow-up call or e-mail sent straight away or a card or free gift for customers at Christmas, it's up to you. It's one of the things that separates companies or people that you 'do business with' with those you really love, respect and feel are part of your life. Feedback can be even more magical. Tell people how well they did. Let them know that you thought their customer care was exceptional. We tend to complain far more than we praise. Not so the soul trader. However, having conversations is not enough. Follow up on that chat at the networking event – the next day. Give a call to that contact you made a few months ago so that you can pick up where you left off. Persist and deliver on what you said you would do. In this day and age when many people have a lot on their plate, lots can easily drop off it. Make a note in the real or virtual diary or in the database, and keep the energy flowing. Never hound; gently remind and check in – maybe things have changed and developed in your contact's business.

Some conversations pay immediate dividends. Some conversations may take months or even years to come to fruition. Some may never emerge. In that way they are like all things in nature. The right environment, nurturing and care will ensure the best results.

Raised profits through conversations

Jez makes promotional videos. We met at a point where he really needed to make a sustainable living from his work. He was networking and had lots of contacts and a knack of meeting all sorts of accomplished people. He had also run a successful business before. But he needed to get focused, so we developed a simple, two-page business plan (which I'll share with you in Chapter 6, 'Creativity'). And he needed to bring in more and better-quality business, so we developed a clear message and conversation for each of these audiences, to bring in more business and to help link them to one another. Jez also needed crew members and a space to work from, so we fed that into our plan too. Jez says: 'At first things were slow. Then business started to pick up. Rash's approach helped lead me to Ravensbourne, a media and incubation hub right next to the O2. Being in this environment has helped my business to generate more work and expand its horizons. This financial year it looks as if we'll double turnover.'

Fast-tracking your business through conversations

Sonali and two of her friends run a soft furnishings business based on traditional Indian designs. Using the clarity, customers, cooperation and conversation themes, in less than a year she took the business from an idea in her head to getting the products into a boutique store. But the importance of conversations became startlingly evident when the owners approached a major trade show attended by major buyers and media – and were rejected. According to Sonali, 'It was all too easy to let go of the opportunity, but I believed that keeping the conversation open and honest would help us. We received feedback that stylized images and stand design were the two aspects we needed to work on.' Spurred rather than deterred, she had conversations and got feedback from contacts, hired a specialist photographer and made tweaks to her website to evoke the high-quality look and feel necessary for the show. Sonali got back in touch with the show organizer. He was impressed that she'd listened, applied his feedback and got back in touch – so much so that he invited them to take part. The event was a huge success, and they have 35 shops, stores and contacts interested. Sonali has conversations at the heart of her strategy, and she is planning to talk to, connect with and meet with them all individually.

Raised profile through conversations

Thierry the yoga teacher has distinguished and high-net-worth clients. During a conversation I suggested we raise his profile through him writing for yoga magazines and attending yoga-related events, because of his unique style, personality and client list. As chance would have it a major yoga exhibition in London was taking place soon after, and he agreed to attend. There he got chatting to the editor of one of the leading yoga magazines and started writing regular articles soon after. Thierry is a great example of someone who – when in the mood – can naturally charm and engage people and who should network more.

If like Thierry you have a strong personality, then it's important that it is harnessed in positive ways. Thierry has had rich conversations, like the one above, that have propelled him forward and others, including with some contacts and suppliers, that have set him back. If you find conversations difficult then make use of the 'Conversation pieces' section at the end of this chapter, which addresses how to get the best from conversations and how to deal with difficult situations.

From cold calls to warm calls

Many business owners hate cold calling – and for good reason: it's often ineffective and irritating. So here is an approach that I call 'warm calls', which I've used since I was that 18-year-old working in media. But I first discovered how effective warm calls can be in business when I attended my first meeting at the London Chamber of Commerce as business coach. I got chatting to another of the new members, who told me he was good at meeting in person but hated cold calling. So I asked him a few questions:

Q: Why don't you like cold calling?

A: Because I feel it's like selling and I don't like selling.

Q: What if you could make a call that wasn't selling?

A: That would be great – I'd far prefer to meet people.

Q: So if you could make calls that were not cold and you simply invited people to a meeting how would you feel and how confident would you be?

A: I'd feel great. I'd be very confident.

I then asked how many meetings he felt he could convert into sales. He replied that it was around 4 in every 10. By the end of our chat he had a huge smile on his face. In a few minutes I had helped him overcome his fears and replace cold calling with a very effective way for him to win business. By the way, each successful meeting he converted into sales would earn him thousands of pounds. Not bad for a free coaching session!

Tom is a teenage entrepreneur who manages a mobile phone apps business. Tom disliked cold calling, which was one of his main marketing techniques. Ringing company after company trying to explain something that they may or may not know or care about can be soul destroying. So I introduced Tom to warm calls. We tweaked his conversations with potential clients – rather than trying to sell apps, he would focus on helping people understand, utilize and take advantage of them. We also stepped up his networking strategy, which plays to his strengths, as he is a sociable young man. This new approach puts him right in his comfort zone.

Who you gonna call?

Perhaps warm calls are something that you could introduce. Interestingly many business owners are nervous about calling their own lapsed or even current customers with whom they may have had a break in contact. One person I know who has a lovely system for making friendly calls is Barnaby. Barnaby runs a marketing company that helps business owners improve their marketing and their pitch to help them become more profitable. He has a bucket in the office with the business cards of all past and present customers. Each week he reaches in and pulls out a card and calls one of the customers and chats. Very often this generates new business. But just as importantly it keeps the conversations going and develops and keeps a strong rapport between him and his customers. It is a brilliant example of the warm call.

Deeper networking

'Deeper networking' is a term I use that is about taking your network to the next level. It is about engaging with your networking contacts more deeply. It is about focusing on the real movers, shakers and business makers in your network. It is about understanding who your ambassadors are. It is about building on the relationship with those people so that you can add value to your business – and theirs. It is about taking time out and fundamentally understanding their business and their ambitions and working together to help each other.

To start deeper networking:

1 Be clear about what you want to achieve.

2 Be clear about the precise bit of business or contacts you want.

3 Identify those in your network who have the connections.

4 Identify those in your network you know, like and trust.

5 Ensure that there is enough good will between you and your contact to lead them to want to help you.

Liz runs a sporting events business. She set it up to marry her passion for golf and sport with running corporate events to help managers team-build, strategize, bond and take time out. However, the economy had taken a knock and so had her bookings. We'd known each other for years through networking, so she gave me a call to see if I had contacts with whom it might be worth putting her in touch. Liz says:

> I've always been a people person. I enjoy networking and think it's one of the best ways to connect and develop business contacts, but I think I may have been missing a trick. The chat with Rash reminded me that I had some great contacts who I should be chatting to more in order to get in front of the right people. This is something that I'm keen to run with: identify my best contacts, connecting with them, seeing who my business can help and having rich conversations. I'm convinced that this will convert into a more profitable business – and that we'll be able to put on more events to thrill, entertain, bond and

de-stress managers. I've already got a few more calls and meetings lined up.

This began a process of deeper networking where Liz and I sat down and explored ways to develop her business further. Among others I introduced her to Neville from Accountagility, a huge sports enthusiast with a background in corporate sponsorship and lots of contacts. It was great timing, as Neville was looking to introduce corporate events for his company.

Deeper networking is a process where you become a key connector, an invaluable part of everyone's network and a true, trusted adviser. In deeper networking there is often a chain reaction of wins well beyond the two people concerned where the circles, influence and reputation of the introducer and contacts involved all benefit.

The hallmarks of deeper networking include:

- ♥ helping those you really like and respect and who provide excellent service for the purpose of helping them and the party you are introducing them to;
- ♥ fully understanding each other's businesses and ambitions;
- ♥ you personally facilitating introductions where two people don't know each other.

Traditional marketing has its place and is important, but deeper networking works profoundly for two reasons: 1) When something is important we often ask someone we know, like and trust. 2) As we've discovered, most small businesses gain most of their business through word of mouth.

Who in your network should you be connecting with and who can you help?

Social media: the conversation generation

We are in the era of conversations. From social networking to business networking sites, there are seemingly endless online communities, discussion forums, blogs and websites. Social networks like Facebook, LinkedIn, YouTube, Twitter and others have revolutionized the way that social and business life is carried out. These media can cause TV talent show unknowns to become superstars overnight through the wave of online views, comments and conversations that follow. Likewise these media can destroy a reputation very quickly when something inept has been said or done and brought to a global audience. In the past you had to have huge marketing budgets to access global platforms. Now individuals and small businesses are at the party. Anyone with online access can have their own video channel, news feed, web page and following. Teenage sensation Justin Bieber was an unknown and gained a following on YouTube. Within a few years he had gained one of the biggest social media followings on the planet. He understands the power of conversation: when his record company suggests an idea he often tweets it to his fans to see what they think. This is savvy – he understands who his customers are and is in tune with them.

This is not just about TV and pop stars on a world stage. One of the attendees of my workshop had spotted this. She ran a swimming club in her local area and put up a Facebook page. The page allowed all those who came along to the club to chat, converse and follow up. It created its own momentum with a few hundred group members, and this happened organically. It meant that the socializing and connections built between local mums and dads and their children could continue between swims.

100,000 followers, zero friends?

Online conversations can be powerful, as can linking old friends and new professional contacts. But many people do not create real connections and trust. Many simply click a button to invite and add 'friends' they've never met. Make your connections real and rich.

> **TIP**   If you link to people via 'friend' or 'business contact' requests, ensure you personalize the message. To me the failure to do so suggests you're lazy or crazy. A personalized, timely message to someone you met yesterday may prove fruitful tomorrow.

Web warning, web wonder

Be very mindful what you post on a blog or comment or complain about online. Think twice about sending that funny tweet – the world can see. Online conversations have an impact and a shelf life beyond any other type of conversation largely because of the power of search engines and the vast networks of people who are linked.

The power of online conversation can be fantastic news if your service is loved and your style is personable. A message sent to your 500 followers is forwarded by one of them, impressed by your wise words or helpful advice, to their 30,000. Be aware that people you've never met and may never meet are being turned on to or off your business by what you say and do online. So the wrong word said – or too many messages sent – may turn someone away from *ever* buying your product or service.

The key is:

1 **Be strategic:** on how every communication ties in with your goals or mission.
2 **Be conscientious:** of the type, volume and impact of communication.
3 **Give good content:** that is of real value to the receiver.
4 **Give it a try:** most businesses try a mix of online marketing and see what fits.
5 **Do what works for you, your customers and your product.**

The art of effective business conversation

Mind your language; watch your tone

One business owner I've worked with shouts at people (without realizing it) when they ring his doorbell. He is not a rude person at all, but he often is caught up in all the busyness of what's going on in the business and in his mind, and if he's not careful people may think him to be a Scrooge character barking at everyone.

Before you speak to anybody, think very carefully about the impact that you want and crucially the result that you want.

The energy with which you conduct the conversation will have a direct result on:

- ♥ the readiness of the listener to listen;
- ♥ the impact of the conversation;
- ♥ the outcome of the conversation and the future potential.

I have at least one business owner who has lost half of the firm's business in less than a week through failing to connect with people in the right way. Years of hard work can go down the drain in minutes if you damage business relationships.

If you employ staff or you have a (virtual) team then the intent, language and tone that you use will either inspire, engage and enthuse them or alienate and infuriate them. How you treat and speak to them will have a direct impact on their motivation and productivity.

Message, medium, money

FIGURE 5.4   How do I reach and keep customers?

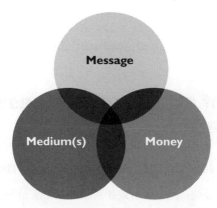

Most of us will need to engage with a whole host of customers, contacts and suppliers during any single week. Each of these interactions is an opportunity to get closer and achieve our mission – so always keep your goal in sight and mind.

Once you know your goal the first thing to be clear on is 'Who is my audience? and then:

1 **What's the message?** Be clear on the specific message that you want to give them, the feeling you want them to get and the result you want.

2 **What's the appropriate medium?** What medium or media will be most effective and most appropriate for them and the situation: call, letter, e-mail, advert, social media, your website, meeting, discussion forum, newsletter? This requires care and trial and error, and getting feedback and the thoughts of savvy contacts will often help.

3 **Where's the money?** Which media actually are most profitable for you? Track exactly where each piece of business comes from so you can tailor your efforts. Ask people how they found you.

Who should be the messenger?
Are you the best person to promote what you do? I've seen many businesses in which the salesperson should be replaced by the customer service rep. Are you and others in your team in the wrong roles? There's no point having the grouch go out to networking events. The best product is worthless in the hands of the worst salesperson. If you're alone in your business you must develop these skills – or bring someone on board who has them. I've seen large and small companies fall at this hurdle. You cannot afford to.

The intelligent 12-year-old test
One of the first things I learnt in the media business was to write (and say) everything as though you were speaking to an intelligent 12-year-old. This holds true in business; ensure everything you say and all your promotional materials are written in this way, which means that they will be:

♥ simple to follow;

♥ jargon free;

♥ succinct;

♥ presented in a way almost anyone will understand.

Say it in a simple sentence

Around 70 per cent of the people I meet ramble, speak jargon, or fail to say what they do in a way that is exciting or memorable.

I want you to write what you do or what your business does in a simple sentence. Aim for a maximum of 10 words.

I remember running a two-day Start Your Business workshop. For a day and a half everyone was speaking jargon, and nobody really knew what others' business ideas were – so how could they help each other? Several, including a pharmaceuticals specialist, gently protested that using only 10 words would be difficult and over-simplistic. But if you can't say it simply you've failed. If the person you meet at the event, who could be or know your ideal customer, can't understand, remember or explain it to others, you've failed.

We did the exercise, and this guy wrote 'I bring life-saving drugs to market.' This was profoundly brilliant. It cut all the jargon and got to the heart of how he helps others. All of a sudden, from one or two of his peers knowing what he did, the whole room knew and were impressed and *moved*, and they would remember him.

Serve, don't sell

The alchemy of converting conversations into business has service not selling at heart. You're changing the entire spirit and dynamic from 'selling' to 'offering' something. It is a subtle but potent shift in mindset, language and approach.

In my early working career I had loads of ideas that I was keen to get my boss to adopt. First I would say 'I think it would be a great idea if...'. Most of the times I used this approach my boss would pass or reject it. Then I changed tack: 'Mike, *do you think* it would be a good idea if...?' This completely changed the dynamic, and I combined it with a change of emphasis: from being bombastic to a wondering kind of tone. It meant that my boss could claim, shape and feel an ownership of the idea. I swiftly learnt that it was better to get the result that I wanted than to take the credit for it!

Over the years I refined this 'serve, don't sell' approach. The fact is that most often we are not interested in buying. We're only interested when we're interested. But when we are looking to serve it is a different ball game. Serving does require attention: you need to understand the viewpoint of the distributor you want to stock your product and the person you want to buy your services.

There is another dimension to this. Why try to push a product on someone who doesn't want to buy? There's no point having long-drawn-out conversations with someone who wants to haggle over price. All the time you are doing this you're missing out on the person who may *want to buy*. Soul traders know their worth and their products and focus their efforts, marketing and conversations on those who would value and benefit.

Transformational conversations

Some conversations have the power to change someone's mind or life. They also have the power to make someone's day:

- ♥ **Spontaneous conversations:** When someone comes to mind whom you haven't been in touch with for a while – a business contact or a customer – call the person. How often have you had a situation when the phone rings and you say to the caller 'I was just thinking about you?'

- ♥ **Personal conversations:** What conversations should you have with friends or family members? It may be about saying 'Thanks' or 'I'm sorry' or to ask for support. If you find this difficult, some of the tools in 'Conversation pieces' at the end of this chapter and in Chapter 7 ('Compassion') will be very useful.

- ♥ **Letting-go conversations:** There may be times when you need to let go of a customer or business or personal relationship that's no longer serving you or them. This is always best done by genuinely wishing them well for the future and speaking from your heart.

- ♥ **Serendipitous conversations:** Life and business are not all about planning. Some things happen when you least expect and you most need them. I recall attending a jazz event in my singing days and having a chat with one of the singers at the end. The singer had a CD called *Serendipity*, and gave me a copy. The singer became my best friend, helped me with my music career and helped inspire and support my work as a coach and speaker.

- ♥ **Life-changing conversations:** One person whose business is based on conversations is Simon. His chequered life as a teenager led from shoplifting and drugs to jail before he changed his life and pursued a career in acting. His work revolves around Simon on the Sofa, an online video channel where he and guests of all backgrounds have what he calls 'transparent conversations' about their lives and life itself. He runs talks and workshops that utilize the same approach to help people develop richer relationships with themselves and the world around them. He says: 'Building the confidence to communicate transparently and knowing I am in control of my own reality has changed my life dramatically and brought with it total abundance of friends, support and wonder', and adds: 'To live a life free from fear, we must communicate our truth.'

Could you be having more open, honest conversations?

Stepping back from conversations

There will be times when there's no value in having a conversation, when it consists merely of counter-productive 'points'. Your ability to be gracious and 'not to go there' will serve you richly. Conversations are usually best had when all parties are calm and when the time, space and energy are conducive.

The power of praise and feedback

We spend too much time finding fault. Give positive, specific feedback to everyone in your life: customers, colleagues, associates, suppliers, and hosts of events. Whilst writing this book I attended a function of the family law firm of Irwin Mitchell Solicitors in London. This team of lawyers are exceptional. They care about their customers, and they run wonderful events to thank their customers and contacts. I told my contact and her team manager *specifically* what I liked and why they were so exceptional. They were all chuffed. The right word can make someone's day and enhance a life.

What conversations should you be having?

OK, I said that this was not a theoretical chapter, so what are the conversations that you should be having? Be mindful of:

- ♥ your life and business goals and aspirations;
- ♥ your strengths, weaknesses, wants and needs;
- ♥ opportunities and challenges;
- ♥ those in your personal and professional network who could help you;
- ♥ past, present and potential customers and contacts.

Now identify the conversations that you will have:

1 Person 1: _____

2 Person 2: _____

3 Person 3: _____

Consider:

- ♥ What are the objectives of the contact and the ideal outcome?
- ♥ What would you like from the contact?
- ♥ What would the other person like from the contact?
- ♥ Key points to discuss in the contact.
- ♥ The best time and means to make the contact (for example, phone, e-mail, letter, online).
- ♥ What is the ultimate win–win here?

Time to review your conversations

1 What tweaks could you make to your website and blog?

2 What changes could you make to enhance your social media?

3 What amendments could you make to boost your other promotional materials?

4 What changes could and will you make to your conversations at home and work?

5 Who would really value a call from you – and who could you benefit from speaking to?

10 new pieces of business

Use Table 5.1 to identify 10 new pieces of business you could gain. If you've been in business for a while also identify 10 pieces of business that you could obtain from former or lapsed customers.

TABLE 5.1 How I can generate business

10 pieces of business that I can generate from old, lapsed and current customers or contacts	Steps I need to take to secure the business (eg call, e-mail, offer incentive, arrange to meet, write mini-proposal, etc)
1.	
2.	
3.	
4.	
5.	
6.	
7.	
8.	
9.	
10.	
10 new pieces of business I can generate	Steps I need to take to secure the business (eg ask client or contact for introduction, call, arrange to meet, e-mail, free or special offer, etc)
1.	
2.	
3.	
4.	
5.	
6.	
7.	
8.	
9.	
10.	

SUMMARY

1 Customer conversion comes from the right customer conversation.

2 Keep all communications clear, crisp, concise and compelling as appropriate to your audience.

3 Psychology: ask, understand and relate; then 'the dance' of possibilities can take place.

4 Identify your conversations: consider the message, medium, money and messenger.

5 Get ready: have something great to say, show, share, sample and serve.

6 Introduce warm calls and deeper networking meetings with key contacts or 'ambassadors'.

7 Use the power of praise, thanks and feedback.

8 Serve, don't sell – and always have the win–win in mind and at heart.

9 Identify 10 pieces of business.

10 Act now: make the calls or contacts and arrange the meetings.

Make use of the 'conversation pieces' here to help.

Conversation pieces

Here are a few tools, tips and techniques to help support and shape your conversations. They work best when you personalize them to fit you, your business and your customers.

Introducing two people

Often we give our contacts a name and leave it at that; we're missing a trick. It is far better that the contact who knows both should introduce them and give a bit of context, so always ask such contacts if they'd be happy to do the introduction. This provides a springboard to kick-start the conversation. Personally I like to call both parties I'm introducing first and then follow it up with an e-mail like this:

FROM: Rasheed Ogunlaru
TO: Elizabeth, Susan
Message flagged
Friday, 2 December 2011, 5.02 pm

Hi Liz and hi Susan

Following chatting to you both today I'm delighted to put you in touch.

Liz: Susan runs Moore VA, which provides support to business and a handful of industry experts. Susan has a pool of associates and a corporate background and some corporate clients. Some of these people or their clients may have a need for corporate hospitality events or refreshing business development days. Susan also supports me as my exec PA and is a great person to have in one's network.

Susan: Liz runs EMG Golf, which provides golf and sporting event management, from arranging golfing events for corporates to providing organizations with boxes and entertainment at major events and bespoke business development events. Liz is a great networking pal of mine and is very personable. I was also thrilled to be a speaker at one of the golf events.

Best wishes, Rash

Following up a meeting by e-mail or letter

When you've had your meeting or met someone at an event, following up is vital to ensure you can turn a conversation into a business relationship:

1 Follow up straight away.

2 Ensure the e-mail or letter is personalized, professional, warm and courteous.

3 Use it as an opportunity gently to highlight ground covered and follow-up actions.

4 Ensure it's the kind of e-mail or letter your contact would like to receive and that it's focused on your contact's agenda.

5 It can work well to accompany the e-mail or letter with a call to alert your contact to it and check receipt.

Here's an e-mail that I sent while writing this chapter to contacts at a university whom I had invited to my workshop. Notice how it starts by saying how pleased you are to have met them, touches on issues that are important to them, gives praise and focuses on future opportunities. Notice how it also offers help and ends by thanking the people who arranged the meeting:

Dear [name]

It was a pleasure to meet you both and to learn more about the excellent initiatives and programmes you're running for students. I'm especially impressed at how mindful you are about the skill set that they will need whether they choose enterprise or employment – and how you reflect that in the programmes you run. I also loved the sound of the experts pool that you're looking to develop. Do keep me in touch – I'd be interested to be involved.

As we also discussed, I'd be delighted to come along and give a talk at the university. I'll add you both to my newsletter as mentioned, and do feel free to add me to your list if/as appropriate. This will help us stay in touch.

On that note please feel free to contact me if I can help further – and your colleagues would be welcome to attend my workshop as my guest if you feel it would be of use. If so simply drop me a line.

Meanwhile thanks [name] again for making this happen.

With best wishes, Rasheed

The reply, which arrived within the hour, was:

Hi Rasheed – thank you so much for your e-mail. You just beat me to it! Thank you so much for a really enjoyable and inspiring workshop, both [name] and I came away with a lot to think about. As we discussed, I can see this fitting in perfectly with what we are trying to achieve, particularly in terms of [detail].

[Name of initiative] is at an early stage – so all the bits and pieces are not quite in place as yet – but I will definitely write as soon as we have got our act together, as it would be lovely to have you involved.

Thank you again.

Giving bad news: dealing with difficult conversations

There may be a range of situations where you need perhaps:

♥ to part company with a client, supplier, business partner or customer;

♥ to make a role redundant;

♥ to pass on some other bad news.

These situations rarely emerge out of the blue. Communication is the breath of every relationship, so ensure that you have a dialogue throughout. If you do, these types of events will be easier to handle and may have been anticipated by all parties.

What tends to make these situations especially difficult is the additional emotional impact and being afraid of hurting others' feelings and the impact on future relationships.

Because of this most people:

♥ avoid and postpone the conversations, which may make matters worse;

♥ take for ever to get to the point, which may annoy the other person;

♥ say it badly or backtrack, which may frustrate you and the other person.

The secret of dealing with these situations is being open, honest and considerate of yourself and the other person. The secret is:

♥ **Step 1: Deliver the message straight away.** 'I'm really sorry but we've decided to end our account with your company at the end of the current contract', 'I'm really sorry but we're going to make your role redundant at the end of your contract', 'I'm very sorry but I've decided to leave our joint venture', or whatever it may be. The point here is that you get the message across that you are leaving, closing the business or whatever the situation is. You say it right at the top of the call/conversation/meeting as apt so that you do not back down, get nervous or get talked out of it.

♥ **Step 2: Focus on the emotion and action you want to leave the person with.** Now that you've said it focus on that person and let the person know that: 'It's been a very difficult decision. You have contributed hugely to what we have done. I'm sorry about this, and I will be providing you with x, y, z' or 'I've learnt hugely by working with you. I really appreciate everything you've done to help build the partnership, but I've decided that I now need to... I'm mindful that we need to address x, y and z. I want to wish you all the best and would be happy to do a, b, c.'

The key thing with step 2 is that it is honest and that you acknowledge the person and the contribution. It can be powerful when you outline what you will do to make the parting sweeter, whether by referring appropriate customers and leads to a business partner you are splitting from or by helping an employee you are letting go with support coaching for the career transition or a top-up on the redundancy payment.

When you do this then most relationships can be salvaged even if the working partnership ends.

Dealing with unwelcome sales calls

One of the top pet hates is unwanted sales calls. Some salespeople are highly trained in keeping you talking and making you buy. Their opening 'spiel' may end with questions to draw you in. If you're not interested, instead of going into the spiral of questions, you may wish to say something like: 'Thanks so much for your call. I'm really not looking for [name of their service] at this time.' They may press you further: 'Thanks again for thinking of my business – but it's really not something for us at this time. Thanks for calling.' You may get the very vociferous caller who doesn't give up so you may have to repeat what you have said: 'Thanks. Unfortunately I have some pressing business so I've got to go now. Thanks for your call. Bye.'

The thing about this approach is that it is warm and friendly. It also doesn't involve lies or deceit: you are not interested in their service at this point and you do have pressing business to get on with: running a business. The final phrase should be accompanied by you ending the call by replacing the receiver.

You'll find your own words and ways of handling such calls; find what works for you.

Dealing with complaints

Complaints need to be dealt with:

- ♥ **promptly** – acting swiftly can nip issues in the bud, but delay will aggravate matters;
- ♥ **professionally** – appropriately, with grace and restraint;
- ♥ **politely** – be courteous and considerate even if the other person is not;
- ♥ **personably** – everyone is an individual;
- ♥ **precisely** – be clear, correct, considered and comprehensive about the points raised.

Top tips are:

1 **Acknowledge.**

2 **Reflect back.**

3 **Say what you can do.**

Dear Mr X

Thank you for your letter of [date]. We note that you were not happy with the quality of the flowers, the delay in receiving the flowers, and being kept on the phone when you complained.

We apologize that you felt that the flowers were not up to scratch. We will refund the cost and we include a voucher for £10 for the inconvenience caused. So sorry that you felt you were kept on the phone for a long time. We noticed in our call log it took about 10 minutes. We're sorry about that. Our team were checking the details and chasing what went wrong. You should have been told what was going on or offered a call back.

You will receive your refund by tomorrow, and your voucher will be with you by the end of the week.

Thank you for bringing this to our prompt attention. We've addressed these issues with our couriers so that it does not happen in future. We strive to offer good service and to make improvement wherever we can. Your feedback has helped us do that.

Yours, Mr Y

Chief Executive

You should have a clear complaints procedure and a process to follow. You should also have the relevant terms and conditions on your website – as well as contracts and agreements where appropriate. Depending on the nature of the issue and complaint there may be other rules and regulations that apply within your industry. In terms of goods or services that are faulty there will also be legislation that covers what you have to do, so you may find that you have to replace or refund even in instances where you may feel it is not appropriate. This is where clear terms and conditions – specific to your company – prepared by a lawyer will be essential.

Small complaints can escalate into drawn-out disputes if you're not careful, which is why being courteous, considered and customer-focused is very important.

Making a complaint: 'Make it professional not personal'

Many people complain when they're in the wrong frame of mind and in a way that may hamper the outcome that they want.

I remember a client who was very late for her coaching session with me because of a faulty bank cash machine that didn't dispense any cash. She went in and complained. However, her mistake was to spend too much time talking about what went wrong and too little about how she wanted the bank staff to put it right.

I Politely, promptly, clearly and succinctly highlight what happened and the problem.

2 Politely, clearly and specifically outline what you'd like the other person to do about it.

3 Be specific: who, what, why, where, when, how, how much and how many?

While you may be annoyed about the situation, be polite and respectful to the people involved. Once situations like this have happened they are past. It's important to focus on the present and to get it sorted out for the future. In some cases you may need to follow a complaints procedure, and you may well need professional or legal advice. It is always advisable to keep a written record for yourself with all the specifics.

Declining a request

No doubt there will be times that you need to decline a request, because for example it's not right – or it's not timely.

Here's a letter I wrote for someone who asked me to write a testimonial on LinkedIn. While I'd met the person two or three times and we had spoken on a one-to-one basis once, I didn't feel I knew the person or their work well enough to write a testimonial.

Dear [name]

I hope you're really well and thanks so much for inviting me to write an endorsement.

It's nice to be thought of. I'm mindful that as we haven't – yet – worked together it would be tough for me to write anything powerful or meaningful and I don't like to write that kind of recommendation. I have no doubt you'd be worthy of a great one so I'd like to wait until we've liaised more or worked on a project together so that I can write something compelling, which I would happily do and look forward to. So please do come back to me on this one in due course and I'd be delighted to.

Thanks, Rasheed.

Postponing or turning down a meeting request

There may be times when someone wants to meet with you but:

1 you're too busy to meet at the moment or in the foreseeable future;

2 you don't want to meet the person at all;

3 you don't have the time to meet in person (but might by phone).

Managing your time effectively as a soul trader is essential, especially if you *are* your business. It is easy to be drawn into everything.

There are a number of options here. One option is postponing: Here's an example of an e-mail I've sent. It would work just as well over the phone:

Thanks so much, good idea. At the moment my diary is very full with work commitments. My diary should clear a little by [give timeframe, allowing extra time for yourself, which may be days, weeks or even months as appropriate]. Do drop me a line then.
With best wishes, Rasheed

You could alternatively tell the person when you will be in contact. It depends on your style, your preference and how important the contact is. If the contact is important I'd give a contact date and put it straight into my diary.

Another option is to meet by phone or online instead:

Thanks so much. That sounds great. I'm quite busy with work here in the office and might be for a while but I'm very keen for us to talk. Could we perhaps arrange a meeting by phone or online?

Keep meetings and calls short and to the point

We've all been there: the phone call or the meeting that is rambling, has no form and never ends. You must be clear from beginning to end:

1 Why are you having the meeting?

2 What specifically do you want to achieve from it?

3 How if at all does it contribute to your business and life goals?

4 When should it take place that is appropriate for all parties and the project concerns?

5 Do you have the time to meet physically?

6 How long should the meeting actually last for?

7 Can you cut down the length of the meeting or agenda to enhance it?

In my experience, most 'general' discussion meetings last for too long, and when they are forced to be truncated because of travel delays and pressing matters they actually become more focused.

Whatever the type of meeting it may be advisable to:

1 have a short, focused agenda sent in advance;

2 have your own agenda bullet points so you stay on track;

3 produce and send bullet points of areas covered and points agreed.

TIP

At times when you're very busy it's wise to make meetings short and succinct, at the start or end of the day so they don't interrupt your day – and to make use of meetings by phone or online systems like Skype to reduce travel times when advisable, appropriate and advantageous.

CREATIVITY

The magic mix of inspiration and action

The true sign of intelligence is not knowledge but imagination.
(ALBERT EINSTEIN)

Never forget to dream – and remember to let your dreams flow into reality...

Everything is energy. We are a manifestation of energy. Business emerges from creative energy. One minute there's nothing; then there's a spark of an idea that in time gives birth to business. But sometimes in all the busyness of running a business, we forget that business is all about this energy and creativity. At one moment, somebody somewhere had the idea for Google, Apple, Facebook and Microsoft – all relatively speaking new businesses. And all of these businesses have blossomed in the internet age – itself a relatively new creation. Imagination and creativity are key components to being an entrepreneur and a soul trader. They are important not just at the ideas and invention stage but every day to continue to develop, compete, create, problem-solve and innovate.

When it comes to being creative and effective, there are broadly speaking two types of business owner:

1 **the dreaming, creative visionary:** strong on vision, passion, drive and creativity but sometimes weak on attention to detail, pragmatism and the framework that is important first to get an idea safely off the ground and then to keep it running smoothly, efficiently and profitably.

2 **the pragmatic, logical organizer:** strong on planning, detail, framework and organizational skills but often weaker on the creativity, flexibility, openness and fun that may be necessary to drive the business forward, keep it innovative and keep the journey enjoyable.

Many business owners have aspects of both, and both aspects are important for you as a soul trader who seeks a successful *and* fulfilling life and business.

This chapter is about helping you achieve the right balance of freedom and framework that will give you the flexibility you need to thrive and that will work for you personally and in business. It will help you:

♥ understand what you're like at your best and how to utilize it;

♥ explore some creative ways that may help you build your business;

♥ develop the right blend of framework and flexibility for you;

♥ consider the financial and people resources you need to develop;

♥ develop a two-page business plan and action plan that work for you;

♥ ensure you have enough fun, balance and creativity at home and work.

This chapter is ultimately about helping you marry your strategic goals with your day-to-day actions in business and to help you stay inspired, focused, motivated, energized, productive and in balance. Many business owners fall down through not being inspired and creative enough on the one hand and not being focused enough on carrying out the right blend of day-to-day activities that will actually help them to move toward their goals and enjoy the journey. In many ways this chapter is a magic box of tips, tricks and tools for you to dip into and for you to use, adjust, develop and apply.

Be at your best

If you were an athlete and I were coaching you, the first thing I'd do is discover what you're good at, your strengths and what works for you. We'd build on it, exploit it and by doing so boost your confidence and ability. Only then would we turn to your weaker areas, tackling them from a position of greater strength and confidence. I'm a huge tennis fan, and many of the greatest players will – as required – 'run around' their weaker wing to hit from their strength. Too many business owners I meet spend too much time on their weaknesses and never fully discover and exploit their strengths. They fail to build the business they could if they played to their strengths and utilized those of others in ways we've already explored that may not cost a fortune – and indeed may not cost a penny.

So let's identify what you're like at your best. In Table 6.1 write 20–25 individual words to describe what you are like at your best. In my case I might have words like *still*, *relaxed*, *calm* and *energized*. Everyone is different; you may need to sit with this for a while and see what comes through.

TABLE 6.1   At my best

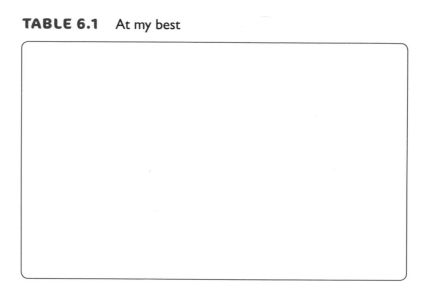

Now in Table 6.2 draw a simple picture of what you are like at your best. It need not be a great work of art. Many clients draw themselves in certain spaces, places or environments, or draw something that symbolically represents them. You may not even know what you're going to draw before you start drawing. That is the magic of the subconscious.

TABLE 6.2   At my best picture

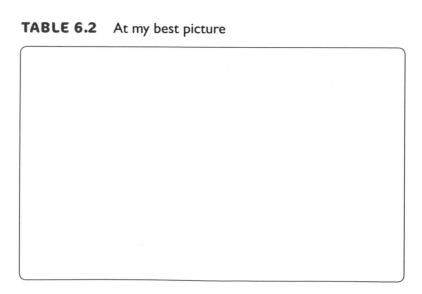

Cast your eye over the words and the picture:

- ♥ What are they telling you about you and your work?
- ♥ How is it that you can use that information?
- ♥ How can you play to those strengths and build on them?
- ♥ How can you use those strengths to address weaker or problem issues?

Your words and your picture will give you useful information about you and your business. They give you clues about when you are most inspired, alive, motivated, enthused and productive. Spending time with and applying this may help you boost your creativity and productivity.

Fit for purpose

During one of our chats it became clear that Susan, who runs the virtual personal assistant business, is at her best when she goes for a run first thing in the morning before work. She becomes energized, starts the day on a high and achieves more. This is very common: I've coached scores of business owners for whom the most powerful thing that we can do to enhance their business performance is first focus on their health, well-being, fitness and life balance. Though very busy, Susan has now prioritized this, and often is joined by a friend – giving them time to catch up before the busy day gets under way.

Creative solutions that work for you

There's a direct link between health and fitness and running a business, and if you *are* your business then you need to ensure that you pay attention to it and take care of yourself. This we will return to in Chapter 7 ('Compassion'). I remember working with an entrepreneur in the property business. His eating habits often affected his confidence, which had an impact on his work. He felt at his best when he exercised first thing in the morning. When he did he ate well and felt buoyant throughout his business day. But he found it very hard to get up in the morning, so I asked him to come up with a creative solution. He decided to put all his exercise equipment and kit downstairs so that it was ready, and then he set up a trail of alarm clocks between his bedroom and the downstairs room where he exercised. It may sound extreme, but it worked for him. Remember, you are the captain of your ship. You need to find the creative solutions that work for you.

Be nurtured by nature

I remember coaching a writer who was struggling with writer's block. She lived in another part of the country, so I coached her by phone. I asked her what she was like at her best. 'When I'm out in nature – it's one of the reasons we moved next to this nature reserve', she replied. However, I discovered her desk was on the other side of the house where there was no view of the reserve. I invited her to move her desk so that she could see the reserve. The results were great; she had a beautiful view to inspire her writing.

Nature, creativity and inspiration are closely linked. It's no surprise, because *inspire* literally means 'breathe'. Maybe you actually need to get more fresh air, oxygen and the nourishment of the sun. This is not mumbo-jumbo. What do you do when you need to clear your head? Remember that we are made of the same water and elements that nature is, so if you are away from nature you're negating your very nature. I like to coach a good number of my clients, especially those who are stuck, outside or away from their offices. In my own case, being still, silent and open – combined with times in nature and with like-minded friends, is where all my ideas and creativity come from.

A new perspective

I remember coaching a successful city lawyer who is managing partner in a busy city practice. She had a full-on working career and huge family responsibilities. We came up with simple, manageable, creative ways of helping her manage her workload and lifestyle.

One of these was moving her desk from the corner of the office, where she felt cooped up, to sitting by the window where she could see out.

Jason is a personal trainer and martial arts expert. He uses parks and a range of creative spaces to train his clients. This means his clients get exercise *and* the fresh air that they need. Having an athlete's attitude, Jason also puts in long hours with his desk work. He realized that after a few hours working at home he becomes less productive, so he now changes his environment every few hours to keep creative, inspired and productive; he works for a few hours at home, a few hours from a business office and sometimes in other environments.

Are you stuck? Do you need a new perspective? Something as simple as moving your furniture around will literally give you a new perspective.

Your dream environment

Graham, the founder of Think Productive, which helps organizations become more organized and effective, practises what he preaches as a business. Life balance and working productively and creatively have always been important to him, so he takes a month out every year to relax and heads to the beach, from where he does his business development, project writing and other work tasks where he is comfortable, inspired, creative and free from distraction.

That's fine on holiday, but Graham became aware that his entire working, home and social environment was important, so during our meetings he mapped out how he and his fiancée might move to the seaside. Within a year they had done it, and now enjoy a better life balance. Graham is more relaxed and is only an hour away from London for key business meetings.

How might you change your working environment so it is more creative and comfortable for you? It might not be about moving home or office, but it might be as simple as putting up an inspiring painting and bringing in a pot plant. If at your best you work well when others are around, might there be more creative and productive spaces that you could work from part of the time like a large library, hotel or gallery?

1 Review your working environment.

2 Have an office clear-out.

3 Rationalize, simplify and systematize your files.

A clean sheet

Forget everything that is happening in your business right now. Imagine none of that is going on. What would be the most effective and productive way to run your business in a way that worked for you, your customers and your life balance? Now write it down and draw it on a piece of paper. Be specific and free-thinking; get creative – see it as a bit of fun.

Now take a look at what you have drawn and written. What things could you apply straight away? What things can you introduce over the next few weeks? What things can you work on over time?

Steve the graphic designer approaches every project this way. He has decades of experience but approaches every piece of work with a clean piece of paper, a clear computer screen and a very open mind. He'll listen to his client's goals and then begin to pull in ideas. He is never bound to any of them, but leaves room for the best result to emerge. By doing so he allows room for everything that he has ever learnt to come through – and in fact he trusts this – but likewise and perhaps more importantly he leaves room for fresh inspiration that brings something special, unique and creative.

The support of a team and working creatively

Perhaps you're at your best when you are with others. Are you isolated and do you work alone? If so, how can you incorporate being around others into your business?

If you have staff or associates, are you getting the best out of them? Do you know what they are good at and what they enjoy doing? In my first job my boss recognized that I loved the work around training people. He was responsible for the TV and radio training programme and let me train as a media trainer and appear on radio and TV as a spokesperson. This boosted my skills, motivation, responsibility and productivity. Find out the strengths and passions of your team and get them to play to them. Like me, they'll become more creative, productive and motivated.

Parit, who runs the reusable bags business, recognized this. He holds team meetings in creative spaces and social events to boost creativity, productivity and morale, and is looking to develop a broader incentives scheme. This is a shrewd move for a growing business, as it means that an inspired, work-hard-but-have-fun culture emerges.

If you have a team of staff, meet them individually, collectively and regularly. Ensure everyone communicates and has a say. Many creative ideas will emerge on how to improve service, and many issues will be spotted early. Don't wait until annual appraisals. Through this you can become more than a manager – you'll be a mentor.

Build your team; build your 'virtual board'

Perhaps, on the other hand, you *are* the business. As we've explored in Chapter 4 ('Cooperation') there are ways you can build your own team. What would work for you? One smart move that many soul traders use is to create a 'virtual board'. At its simplest – and often most powerful – you identify professionals in and through your network who have skills that you might need, and you help support each other's businesses to grow. So Zestworks, the collaborative group that I was involved in, was like a virtual board. There was the coach (myself) and marketing, finance, legal and HR specialists. We all ran our own businesses, helped each other individually and called on each other when we needed each other's expertise. Sometimes virtual boards last for a long time; sometimes they change or disband. If yours is a growing business then you probably need people who have been at finance, marketing and operations director level to help you. You want people *at least* as talented as you in their own fields. Many great entrepreneurs say that they seek those who are better than they are. Seek out the exceptional people. Whilst they'll have different strengths, styles and skills, ensure that they share your values. If they do not there will be discord and disharmony, and the group will probably disband. Remember, as probably nobody is getting paid, it is the shared values that will bind you together.

Thierry, the yoga teacher who is producing a new fitness product, would benefit from creating a virtual board. For him, having an accomplished marketing and PR expert, someone with a background in fitness products and the industry, could pay huge dividends, help avoid pitfalls and lead to contacts. This virtual board model is something that David the car parts entrepreneur has begun to develop. He has a virtual operations director: a retired former colleague who was an operational director. He's now seeking a finance and a marketing expert. The beauty of virtual boards is that, if you get the right person with the right heart, then they may well turn into 'real' members of your business over time. This is what happened in Robert's finance software business. He met Neville, an experienced marketing and business development expert, at a time when Neville was looking at his next steps. This is a simple example of the power of thinking creatively and being open combining with the themes we have already covered to pay dividends.

Gain value with virtual assistants

Getting a virtual assistant can be a creative way of increasing your capacity without needing to hire someone. You don't need to have the desk space, as virtual assistants work remotely, and they tend to have differing strengths and expertise, so you can find one with the kind of skill set that might work for you. I asked Susan, the former Virtual Assistant of the Year, for some tips on getting started with a virtual assistant.

10 top tips for working with a virtual assistant

1 Identify the three tasks you'd love to delegate.

2 Ask for recommendations for a virtual assistant from your contacts.

3 Prepare a brief – be clear what you'd like support with.

4 Set your budget.

5 Telephone interview: does the person have the right skill set and experience?

6 Working style: when and how do you work?

7 How do you like to communicate – e-mail, telephone, occasionally face to face?

8 Check financials and 'legals': fees, contract, insurance, data protection registration.

9 Invest some time in your virtual assistant: what are your objectives and who are your key contacts?

10 Regular communication – diarize regular calls so that you're both up to date.

Thank you for the music

Music can help boost creativity and productivity. It's no surprise factories, offices and shops have music playing to raise the spirits of the workforce and customers. Many people find gentle classical music, for example, very effective, and it is often used strategically to boost creativity, calm people down and soothe the mind. Some of Mozart's music has often been cited and applied for its soothing qualities, for example. See what music works for you and those you work with. I'm a big fan of Radiohead and have their music on in the background when I have writing work to do. Three albums in particular are just mellow enough with the vocals just subtle enough to support what I'm doing but not distract me. That's the key: that the music adds but does not distract. However, there will be other times when silence is the best sound, and if you tend to be 'noisy' then silence may be worth introducing.

Use your time and energy wisely

Good timing is everything

What time are you at your best? Maybe like me you're at your best between 6 and 9 am, and they are your most creative and productive hours. Perhaps early evenings are when you're most fresh. How can you change things so you can utilize your best times?

I'm a big tennis fan, so a few years ago a few weeks ahead of the Wimbledon championships I drew a line in my diary at midday for those two weeks, indicating I would stop working then. I used a colourful highlighter pen to mark out this time, and it felt great doing so. I made sure all my meetings and work were scheduled for the morning. For that fortnight I was as effective – if not more so – because I was more focused up till noon and knew the rest of the time was mine. I now often employ this method.

There may be portions of the day where you're ineffective, and there may be no value you trying to do certain work at those times. If you know you slouch in the afternoon put in simple tasks then that you know you'll achieve. Study your patterns and be honest with yourself about when you're at your best and worst. When I worked in the media I often worked insanely long hours and skipped lunch, often starting earlier and leaving later than others. This is madness – it is not effective. After 2 pm I was not productive at all. Are you kidding yourself in your business? What do you need to change?

If you have staff, look at this creatively and flexibly. Who is on your team, and when are they each at their best? You may well improve your entire business by doing this. If you currently open your business from 9 am to 5 pm but discover some work best from 7 am to 3 pm and others from 11 am to 7 pm you've just made yourself, your staff and your customers very happy and added a selling point to your business. It requires the courage to go against convention if need be. Suzanne's business is US based, and most of her clients are in the UK. She splits her day into two so that she can get on with some of her admin work when her customers are asleep, whilst much of her work with customers can be done at any time and simply requires e-mail contact.

- ♥ What times of the day are you best for strategic planning?
- ♥ What times of the day are you best for administrative and operational tasks?
- ♥ What times of the day are you best for marketing and promotional talks?
- ♥ What times of the day are best for you to have meetings?
- ♥ What times of the day are you not good at?
- ♥ What changes can and will you make, and when?

Whatever you do it is essential that you put in time out and lunch. If you don't take a break, you may break.

Time to start managing your energy

Being mindful of time is one thing, but time is finite. If you say things like 'There are not enough hours in the day', stop. You can't control the number of hours in the day, but you can change your relationship with time. Interestingly, when you change your relationship with time you find that you utilize it wisely and move beyond it being your reference point. You can move to focusing your energy on what is important.

We talk a lot about managing our energy consumption at home and work, but we rarely think about it in terms of those things that drain or boost our own energy:

- ♥ What are you spending most of your energy on?
- ♥ What are the things and who are the people who boost your energy?
- ♥ What are the things and who are the people who drain your energy?

Write the answers down. I remember coaching a dress and jewellery maker who found certain people draining – she needed to let them go from her life in order to let in those with more enriching energies and possibilities. She found museums and galleries inspired her creativity. By spending more time in those spaces she became more productive and met new people who were on her wavelength. It may be that certain products, projects or even clients are no longer serving you, and you need to let them go with a kind heart. You listen to your stomach when you are hungry, so listen to your instincts and motivation levels when they're telling you things aren't working.

Managing and nurturing your creativity

Ideas boxes

Take a look at the three boxes in Table 6.3 and give yourself the time and the space to put in all your ideas. These can relate to every aspect of your business and wider life. It may include new ways of working or new product or service ideas. It could be ideas to improve profits, your life or customers' experience – or a new venture or adventure for your life. Go for it; you're simply giving yourself the room to get ideas out of your head on to the page. If you are very creative, why not get yourself three actual boxes and write and put the ideas in them? At this stage you are just having fun and allowing yourself to create. Just as kids learn and develop through play, it's important to give yourself room to plan, explore and grow.

1 **Good ideas:** Put in everything that you think would be a good idea. Don't edit yourself; capture the ideas. Maybe there have been ideas you've had for years; maybe new ones will emerge.

2 **Challenging and courage-taking ideas:** Maybe these are the kinds of ideas that would push your comfort zone. They may require some time, support and attention. Maybe you've had them in mind for years – let them out. These may include diversifying or changing, increasing prices, hiring staff,

TABLE 6.3   Ideas boxes

Good ideas

```
┌─────────────────────────────────────────────────────────────┐
│                                                               │
│                                                               │
│                                                               │
│                                                               │
│                                                               │
└─────────────────────────────────────────────────────────────┘
```

Challenging ideas

```
┌─────────────────────────────────────────────────────────────┐
│                                                               │
│                                                               │
│                                                               │
│                                                               │
│                                                               │
└─────────────────────────────────────────────────────────────┘
```

Crazy ideas

```
┌─────────────────────────────────────────────────────────────┐
│                                                               │
│                                                               │
│                                                               │
│                                                               │
│                                                               │
└─────────────────────────────────────────────────────────────┘
```

relocating, getting or letting go of an office, teaming up with others or entering a new market.

3 **Crazy ideas:** List them, however ludicrous. Just go for it. What things might other people do in your shoes? What would be the most amazing thing that you could try to achieve? Some crazy ideas are the most powerful ideas.

Now take a look at these ideas. There may be some 'no-brainer' ideas you can introduce quickly and effectively with little time and money and few risks. Other ideas may be worth sleeping on. Often the good measure of a great idea is how strongly it stands up in a day, week and month from now.

The questions below will help you consider and develop your idea. As a soul trader you must learn when to run with an idea, when to develop and test it and when to stop yourself.

- ♥ What will be involved from idea to delivery? (List everything: time, energy, resources. Be specific: what, when, how many, how much?)
- ♥ What further information, help and expertise do you need to consider this idea?
- ♥ What will be the costs involved?
- ♥ How will you continue to run and fund your business while involved in this project?
- ♥ What are all the risks and what might go wrong before, during and after?
- ♥ What might happen if you are successful?
- ♥ What might happen if you are unsuccessful?
- ♥ What has been your track record on previous ideas and have they paid off?
- ♥ How can you safely test the idea to see if it is viable?
- ♥ How can you test if there is actually a demand for your idea?

With big ideas it is especially essential to consider how you will continue to run your business and generate a profit while you are developing your idea. I cannot stress this enough. I and many soul traders have suffered through not being mindful of that.

Magical marketing mix

In all the day-to-day work of running a business you can forget actually to bring the business in – or get stuck with tried-and-tested means.

100 means of marketing and promotion

Let's see if you can list 100 differing ways of marketing and promoting your business within 60 minutes. Take a piece of paper and divide it into two columns with these headings: 1) 50 free/nearly free ways; and 2) 50 paid-for methods. There may be crossover with the ideas boxes exercise that you completed in Table 6.3, and you may want to revisit your notes from other chapters of the book too. You might list things like word of mouth, business cards, adding customer testimonials on your website, leaflets and so on. You might add more ambitious or interesting things like exhibitions, affiliate programmes and events, and product launches. You may find that you have several initiatives that spring from one specific marketing tool, for example: 1) create a social media page; 2) add a monthly free offer for one of your products on that page; and 3) add an events list to the page.

If you get stuck then consider what others in your industry and other industries do. Add things that you feel you'd like to do but are too scared or unsure to do or don't know how to do. Include things that other marketing-savvy businesses do. This is all part of being creative and letting the creativity flow.

Somewhere in here are *at least* a handful of very practical and valuable ways of building on your marketing. The great thing is you may discover some ideas that you can employ now and others for when your business grows or finance allows.

Two-page business plan

Let's now make use of all this information and this creative space to write your two-page business plan. You may have begun following Chapter 1 ('Clarity'); if so, now's a good time to review and fine-tune it. Or if you've read through the book then now is a good time to pull all that information and inspiration together.

Business plans are written for two purposes and for two audiences: 1) for you to identify who and where you are, where you're going and how you'll get there; and 2) for investors or funders for the same purpose. If you're seeking funding from others then you'll need a longer, more detailed business plan with detailed information on you, your team, your product, the costing, and your marketing and promotional plan. Your plan also needs to outline the financials: costs, projections, sales to date, break-even points and so on. I've included some tips on funding for growth in the section 'Playing it smart with business funding and growth' (p 196).

If you're not seeking funding you may not need a weighty business plan, but it may well still be useful producing a plan with a lot of the specifics such as this. I found that most people who've written a business plan look at it at the start of their business, then file it and rarely if ever read it again. If so, what's the point of having the plan? Meanwhile many plans are so unwieldy that even the business owners are bored by them. This is insane. You must be inspired by your business plan.

I'm inviting you to write a two-page business *and* action plan. It will be a strategic and a practical creative tool. Instead of being a dry, lifeless document it will be an alive one. The secret is to keep it short, sharp, succinct and specific. See it as being like giving someone a very specific address of where you are going and then very specific directions on how to get there. Keep the intelligent 12-year-old in mind whilst writing. This needs to be the kind of thing you (or others) could pick up, understand and run with.

Table 6.4 is the two-page business plan template. There are tips on how to complete it immediately afterwards.

Page 1

- ♥ **Who you are:** Summarize this in a short punchy sentence.
- ♥ **Your mission:** Summarize in one to two inspiring and specific sentences.
- ♥ **Products/services:** Bullet-point your main products or services in a way anyone can understand.

One- to five-year goals

- ♥ **Finance:** What are your financial goals? Write them specifically: 'Year one I want to make X thousand, year two I want to

TABLE 6.4 Two-page business plan

Who I am/we are:
Mission:
Products/services:
Goals (1–5 years) Finance: Marketing: Operations/management:
Marketing blend/plan:
Key performance indicators:

TABLE 6.4   *continued*

Strengths:		Weaknesses:	
Opportunities:		Threats:	
Action plan			
Operations:	Marketing:	Finance:	

make Y thousand and year three I want to make Z thousand.'
Think very carefully about the basis on which you're
setting those particular financial goals. In most cases it's
a combination of what we feel is achievable and a little bit
of aspiration.

♥ **Marketing:** What are your specific marketing-related goals?
It may be that you have a clear number of particular customers.
Put down the number and type. You may even have specific
names. You may also want specific marketing-related tools
in place – website, promotional materials and so on. Write
it down and the target date. Like Sonali you might want to
exhibit in a specific show or be stocked in certain shops.
Have these marketing things in place by the target date.

♥ **Operations:** What are the management- and operations-
related goals that you want to have for your business for
the next 1–5 years. Perhaps like Graham of Think Productive
you want to bring in specific staff. Be clear about your role
and theirs. Again write it in short bullet points: 'Admin
assistant by December 20XX'. Perhaps you want to bring in
somebody to help you to do your marketing or your admin
by year two or what have you. What are those goals?
Bullet-point them specifically.

♥ **Marketing blend:** Bullet-point the blend of differing
marketing and promotional means that you envisage using
to achieve your above goals. This is likely to include the
key items or the best ideas from the marketing mix exercise
(p 178) and the ideas boxes in Table 6.3 and from
Chapters 2 ('Customers') and 4 ('Cooperation').

♥ **Key performance indicators:** How will you know if you're
on track? Put in some indicators of how you'll know you're
performing and moving toward your goals. These may relate
to sales, customer service, output or anything else. For
example: 'Convert one in three meetings into a paying
customer; have one in 10 website visitors buying at least £20
of products; and achieve 90 per cent customer satisfaction
with our product.' How will you measure all this?

Page 2

SWOT (strengths, weaknesses, opportunities, threats)

Hopefully you did this in Chapter 1 ('Clarity'). If so, add it in and add anything else that's emerged. Be as specific and exhaustive as you can.

Action plan

This part of the two-page business plan is very important indeed. Many people have 'to do lists' but often fall down because these lists end up being too 'day-to-day' and are not closely enough linked to your overall strategic goals. The secret of completing this is first to revisit your specific strategic goals on page 1 and then to ask yourself: 'What do I need to do in terms of my operational, marketing and finance actions in order to achieve it?' The action plan will have some very specific actions such as 'Call John on Monday the 3rd to add a new "About Us" web page by Friday the 30th.' It needs to be so specific that anybody could pick it up and follow it as an instruction. Again the key is to keep it short, sweet and succinct. Typically the actions on the two-page business plan tend to cover the next three to six months or so. It all depends on the nature of your business. Be disciplined with yourself; ensure it ties in with your specific goals. In the event that you are changing focus or looking to raise your game, many of your actions may be focused on finding out information, researching, meeting key contacts and asking them for information, and very specific meetings. Here are a few of the kinds of things you might have on your list just to give you an idea.

Operations

- ♥ Complete two-page business plan by 15 January.
- ♥ 20–30 January: research new cheaper phone company and switch by 1 March.
- ♥ Ask Mark and Maggie about virtual assistants by 15 March and hire one by 1 June.

Marketing

- ♥ 5 January: write newsletter and e-mail with new half-price January sale offer.
- ♥ January: speak to Fred about creating a new customer database by 30 January.
- ♥ 20–30 January: call five main clients to wish them Happy New Year and arrange meetings.
- ♥ February–March: update customer database and complete by 20 March.
- ♥ February–March: research and join two to four appropriate networking groups for my sector.
- ♥ February–March: meet five identified ambassadors with the aim of securing new contract.

Finance

- ♥ 10–20 January: organize all invoices and update price list.
- ♥ 15 February: transfer 25 per cent of takings into savings account ready for tax bill.
- ♥ April–May: meet three new accountants and select by end May.
- ♥ June–August: research setting up pension plan for the company.

Living with your two-page business plan

This is a living document. Use it. Personalize it; be creative. Have it where it's very visible: on your desk, on your notice board, at the front of your main business file. Carry it around with you – whatever works for you. I recommend that once a week you take 10 minutes:

- ♥ to refresh yourself on your goals;
- ♥ to update the action plan;

♥ to review anything related to the strategic goals;

♥ to add any specific follow-up actions in your online or paper diary.

I don't want to be too prescriptive about this, as the secret is that you do what works for you, but as with any habit it's worth spending a few months doing it regularly so that it becomes part of your being and you work with it your way. The aim is to internalize and memorize it so it gives you creative flexibility. You may move to a point where you have no more need for this action plan, as you are living it. There may be other times when you may wish or need to reintroduce it.

Getting to grips with your year

Most businesses have cycles or routines within their business year. Your work may be seasonal, where there are peak seasons and lulls. You may have key finance, marketing or operational issues to address at regular times. It's one of the reasons that many large companies divide the year into quarters, so that they can financially and strategically plan. By keeping your eye on the big picture you can start to get creative about how to address those issues. Jason the personal fitness trainer knows that lots of clients want to get fit in January as the New Year starts and that the schools he works in are on holiday from July to August and this may be a quieter time. Using this information he has started to plan his entire year. He also created some great initiatives for schoolchildren targeted for the summer holidays that address both a traditional quiet time in his business and a time that these youngsters might best benefit from activities to keep them active, engaged, energized and out of trouble.

Take a look at Figure 6.1 and consider your business. Month by month consider the main issues and trends that relate to *finance*, *marketing* and *operations*. Perhaps you can schedule in when you need to complete tax bills, set up marketing campaigns in good time, carry out operational tasks, and so on. Then take a look at

FIGURE 6.1 Plan, preview, perform, review and improve

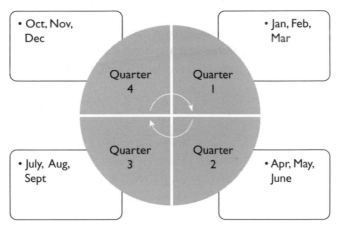

- Oct, Nov, Dec

Quarter 4

- Jan, Feb, Mar

Quarter 1

- July, Aug, Sept

Quarter 3

- Apr, May, June

Quarter 2

each quarter as a whole, and you may wish to set a few simple goals. Let's imagine that – such as in Jason's business – the summer months (quarter 3) are quiet. If so you may wish to set specific financial targets (linked to marketing activity to achieve it) for quarters 1 and 2 in order to have the cash you need for quarter 3. So once again take a look at your year as a whole and in quarters and ask yourself:

- ♥ What are the main patterns?
- ♥ What are the key challenges and priorities to be addressed each quarter?
- ♥ What needs to be achieved by the end of each quarter?
- ♥ How can you most creatively capitalize on busy times and utilize quiet times?

There are all sorts of simple things that can be done to get the best out of your year once you understand the patterns.

TIP Does it go quiet in mid-December? I invite my clients to book in meetings or calls with key customers and suppliers for early in January to get the next year off to the best start – or you can use it to plan your year ahead.

The tools and tricks that you use

There are all sorts of tools to help you manage your business, from computer software and smartphone apps to diaries and year planners. Be creative, use what works for you, tweak and tailor.

Get creative

If you find traditional year planner charts don't quite fit your business, create one of your own or research one that fits you. Experiment; explore what others in your network use. But, just because everyone else has all the latest technology, don't feel that you have to if it doesn't work for you and your business. Warren Buffett, the acclaimed billionaire entrepreneur and philanthropist, uses simple systems and a sharp instinct. However, if you know some new tools and technology could help, get someone you trust to set you up on the system and train you. Ensure technology empowers and enables – and does not trap, distract and confine you.

I use a range of old and new tools. I use a traditional week-per-view diary so I can see at a glance how busy I am or wish to be. I like the fact that I can touch the page and 'work with it'. As far as marketing is concerned I'm aware promotional methods change all the time, so I stay in touch with those in my network who are more aware of the tech and social media aspects. I'm therefore in touch and adopt the things that work for me – and I get my tech contacts to help set up my accounts. I'm creative and visual, so producing products and using visual forms of marketing like videos for online promotion sit well with me. Again it's important to know your strengths and those within your 'team'; if one person is great with technology and another is great with marketing and another is great with administration then you are on to a winner.

What do you need to create or find?

So where are you at right now? Are there gaps that need to be addressed? What things do you need to create in order to move your business forward? Perhaps there are skills you wish to develop or people expertise that you wish to bring in. Identify these things and add them into your business or action plan.

Lesley is a client I'm working with on her health and well-being business. She has details of various contacts and leads, but they're not organized, so she has the task of developing a database containing all her client, lead and supplier details. This is on the action plan page of her two-page business plan – as is asking trusted people in her network who may know a specialist to help her set up her database. She is also about to set up a simple desk and computer filing system that works creatively for her.

Arguably the most important quality of being an entrepreneur is being resourceful. A soul trader cannot afford to dwell on what's not going right and problems. A soul trader embraces the situation as it is and asks 'How can this be addressed?' and 'Who can help me and how can I help that person in return?'

What could you create?

Earlier in this chapter we looked at creating ideas boxes (Table 6.3) and the marketing mix. Thinking about everything that we've covered in this book – your aspirations, your journey, your customers, your mission and your industry – what is it that you could create? Is there something that has your name on it? Is there something that could be developed and built?

Thierry the yoga instructor realized that there was a personal fitness product that he could create, and he is now developing it. It's been a tough journey. He's had to find designers and developers, learn about patents and design rights, and assemble a team, but it is something he is passionate about.

Donald the surveyor has developed his own unique, user-friendly reports, and these have been incredibly popular with clients. He is now looking at other resources he might create for his peers and customers. In my case my own 'Become who you are' style of coaching emerged over time from my own unique journey, my skill set and what I found my clients were actually experiencing. It was only when I really began to embrace my own hybrid style that things unfolded naturally for me. Since then I've created talks, downloads, books and a video product to help serve my clients and develop my business.

There may be all sorts of products and possibilities that you have. It may be a mass market product or it may be about revamping your tools and materials to give them a personal touch.

Managing the day-to-day

Now that you've developed your two-page business plan and have explored how to manage your time and energy, it's important to consider what's going to help you achieve your goals and stay creative. If you're quite organized you may already have this covered – but, if you're awash with ideas, too unstructured, easily distracted or inefficient, the life and business planner exercise with its timetable shown in Table 6.5 may be useful.

TABLE 6.5   Rasheed's 10-minute life and business organizer – time, energy, tools and team

> *The three keys to your success:*
>   1. Clear, compelling, specific goals and the mindset and behaviour to go with them.
>   2. Develop the team, resources and skills to achieve your goals.
>   3. Manage time and energy wisely.
>
> *Complete in brief bullet points:*
>
>   Mindset required:
>
>   Habits/behaviour required:
>
>   Environment required:
>
>   My key output/key performance indicators:
>   Yearly:
>   Monthly:
>   Weekly:
>   Daily:

TABLE 6.5   *continued*

Top tips:
  1. Two-page business plan or weekly review: Introduce a 10-minute
     weekly review of progress; update and set actions.
  2. Meetings: Make them half the time; aim for a one-hour maximum.
     Introduce phone or online meetings.
  3. Computer: Clear desktop. Have three to five main files, eg finance,
     marketing, ops and prospects, with subfolders.
  4. Calls: Set a limit. Use answering machines or staff. Keep calls focused
     and to the point.
  5. E-mail: A big distraction. Clear folders. Set up and use replies.
     Have start and end times, eg 10–11 am. Close to avoid
     distraction.

My team (name/role):
  Additional support needed (role/when):
  Delegate (task/to whom/when):
  Skills, training, education needed (and when):
  Tools and technology needed (and when):

Best times for each task:	Energizers:
Strategic planning:	
Finance:	Drains:
Marketing/sales:	
Operations/admin:	Distractions/interruptions to manage:
Calls:	
Meetings:	People to educate/communicate to:
Product development:	
Other:	New habits/routines needed:

Daily timetable:

Morning	Lunch/breaks	Afternoon
6 am		1 pm
7 am		2 pm
8 am		3 pm
9 am		4 pm
10 am		5 pm
11 am		6 pm
12 noon		7 pm

TABLE 6.5 *continued*

Weekly timetable:

Time	Mon	Tue	Day Wed	Thurs	Fri
6 am					
7 am					
8 am					
9 am					
10 am					
11 am					
12 noon					
1 pm					
2 pm					
3 pm					
4 pm					
5 pm					
6 pm					

Creating the right business model for you

We're now at the point in this book where it's about shaping your business in a way that delivers for you and your customers: financially, personally, professionally and if you like spiritually. If we look at franchise businesses as an example, there's a clear model that has been created. Everything is clearly defined, from the brand and marketing right through to the equipment, systems, processes and service. Your business aspirations and personal style may not require such a degree of structure, but it's worth exploring what framework your business needs to ensure it runs effectively and profitably.

One factor may be the kind of entrepreneur you are. Broadly there are two types:

1 **The equity entrepreneur:** You're in a business with the idea of building, scaling and possibly selling it. You may be dealing with physical (or virtual) products or a replicable service. Building a profitable business that can run without reliance on you is vital. Very often there are other investors or stakeholders, which is why the term 'equity' is relevant.

2 **The lifestyle business:** You've set up a business and a living based around your skills, passion, life values and priorities. The focus is not usually – initially at least – about building a business to scale. Very often the lifestyle entrepreneur will always be the only employee of the business.

Many 'business purists' say a lifestyle type only becomes a business if and when you can take the owner out of the equation and the business could still run in terms of staff, systems, sales and cash flow. I'm not a purist and apply the term 'business' wherever there is enterprise, and the term 'business' is useful to ensure that you're running a 'businesslike' venture. However, the test of whether your business could run effectively without you raises tough and valuable questions for every type of business owner. This in itself might help you consider what your business model might need to look like now, in a few years and in the longer term.

Most traditional soul traders are lifestyle business entrepreneurs – or start out as such. The equity business owner should consider business models from the outset, as the goals and logistics involved mean that the management, structure, systems, staffing and marketing need a clear focus, path, cash flow and exit plan – especially if there are other business partners or investors involved. In fact it's best understood by looking at it as if you had been asked to invest in someone else's business. You'd want to know how it was managed, run, funded and marketed and what the financials and financial prospects were.

Whilst there are two types of business owner, these are two ends of the same line, and increasingly I meet lifestyle soul traders who want to make more of an impact, spread their wings and perhaps introduce new products and services or who are now running social *enterprises*. Once this happens you need to think about how you can best make this sustainable. Equally, I am meeting more equity entrepreneurs who suddenly are asking themselves questions about who they are, their lifestyle and what they want to contribute.

Many soul traders are bringing the best of both business styles together. There's an opportunity to be creative and to shape a business model – or break the mould – in a way that delivers in financial, strategic, emotional and spiritual terms.

Do you have the right foundations in place?

Heather understands the challenges of creating the finance, management and operational structure. Born and raised in the United States, she had a successful career in finance and operations before moving to the UK to set up Back Office Support Solutions, a business helping businesses with their finance and management. We met through our contacts and became team mates at Zestworks.

Here are her top 10 tips:

1   Open a separate bank account for your business, even if you are a sole trader. All money in and out for the business should go through this account, no matter what – seriously.

2   Get in the habit of keeping your receipts for *everything* – better to have receipts for expenses that you may not be able to claim than not having receipts for valid business expenses and therefore paying too much tax at the year end.

3   Put the critical reporting dates in your diary *now* (the bare minimum is: annual return due date, annual accounts due dates and corporation tax due date for limited companies, and self-assessment tax return and payment due dates for sole traders). (There are other dates for payroll and VAT reporting, but they will not apply to everyone.)

4 Get your clients to sign a contract or at least e-mail a confirmation of work to be done with an agreed price *before* you start work. This is not 'mean' and 'too formal'; this is polite and professional.

5 Start chasing late payers *right away* – do not wait until invoices are very overdue. The first call or e-mail can be to ask if they have received the invoice and if there are any questions on it. The second one can be to check if payment has been made, as the due date has just passed. Some people only pay those who pester them, so do not stay quiet.

6 Resist the urge to over-service your clients. They will get used to it very quickly and will expect the same level of service for no extra cost for the rest of your relationship with them.

7 Resist the urge to price yourself too low – but, if you must to start out, increase it as soon as you can. A letter to your existing clients saying 'Our prices have been £50 an hour for all new clients for the last three months, but as you are such a valued client we are only increasing your fees from £30 to £40 per hour.'

8 Profitability is *not* the same as cash flow. For instance, what is in your bank account is not necessarily what you have to spend. Put at least 25 per cent of all your sales receipts into a savings account to pay for the eventual tax that you will need to pay.

9 Do not be afraid to register for VAT early (unless you sell to consumers), and use the advantages of the flat rate scheme (appropriate for UK businesses) for as long as you can.

10 There is nothing wrong with bartering your services in the early days to get your first few customers. Just be sure that they at least give you a testimonial that you can use on your website or that you can talk about the work you do for them to other potential customers.

HEATHER'S TIP

'Don't be stuck doing things like everyone else is doing them – for instance, why not price your services based on the value you bring to the customer, not on the number of hours worked? Why not give everyone a discount for paying by credit/debit card instead of putting a higher fee on these payments? You could demand payment up front by card and then never have to deal with chasing late payers ever again – that is worth a 2 per cent discount, no? Why not give limitless commissions instead of capping them? Share a bit of the wealth with those that helped you get it. Why stay open from 9 to 5? Why not announce your hours to be 10–6 or 8–4 – as long as people know what they are, they can manage accordingly. Being creative is about setting your own business rules, but not being totally ruled by them.'

Playing it smart with business funding and growth

Perhaps like several people in the book you're looking to start, grow or expand or develop new products in a way that requires funding.

Paul Grant is a soul trader and entrepreneur who set up his business, The Funding Game, to help businesses understand and raise finance through events and advice clinics. He also works alongside many business angels (established entrepreneurs who invest in new businesses). I asked him for his top tips for raising finance shrewdly and creatively:

Many entrepreneurs waste a huge amount of time raising start-up capital. However, when you understand the rules of the funding game the chances of success dramatically increase. There are all sorts of challenges involved in raising funding for a business at start-up and growth stages and all sorts of factors to consider. What's more, there are all sort of myths involved, such as you must have an extensive, robust business plan to raise capital.

Paul's top 10 tips for raising and managing finance are:

1 **Get really clear what you need the funding for:** Is it for staff, premises, product development or marketing? Each can be financed differently, and many do not even need funding.

2 **If you are at the start-up stage:** Consider working part time or offering consultancy initially to support the enterprise; then take a look at help from family and friends, your own savings, grants and local incubators. Above all, use whatever contacts and resources you have to make some early sales.

3 **If you are at the growth stage:** You may want to consider a new trend of 'crowd funding' such as crowdcube.com and then business angels, banks (stick to overdrafts), corporate credit cards (not personal credit cards), extending credit terms with suppliers, invoice discounting and, if you are going for super-fast growth, venture capitalists.

4 **Angel investors:** These are high-net-worth individuals who have enough cash to take a chance with high-risk, early-stage investments. They are interested in opportunities that offer a chance to return 10 times their original investment.

5 **Angel investors are looking to invest in companies that have an experienced team**, a strong idea, an effective marketing plan, the chance of an exit, sensible valuation and ideally some early sales indicating an appetite for the product or service.

6 **Venture capitalists:** These are organizations that use other people's money, including pension funds and private companies. Like angels they also want 10 times their return on investment, but the deal size is much higher and starts from £2 million. There is also an extreme pressure to sell their stake in a trade sale or float shares on the stock market within five years. They are worth considering if you have proven the concept in at least one market, are highly scalable, and have an all-star team.

7 **Managing your money:** The key thing is to understand cash flow and other financials such as your break-even point, cost

of sales, average sale value and net profit. Remember, an accountant is about recording what has happened, not predicting the future in forecasts. You also should think about keeping fixed costs as low as possible, such as office lease, staff on payroll, and vehicles.

8   **The right team** is critical. Most investors know that the business plan will change. It will then be down to the team to show the creativity and resilience to find another way to make the business a success. The ideal team consists of a marketing director, a product, technical and operations director, and two experienced non-executive directors who have a mentoring role.

9   **Common wisdom** in the media is to use *all* your savings in your new venture. I believe you should look at your own business as an angel investor would. Angel investors would never put all of their capital into one venture but would spread the risk over 6–10 ventures. My advice would be to put in 25 per cent. Keep another 25 per cent on hold in case the business runs out of cash. Then whatever happens keep the remaining 50 per cent as a safe house.

10   **Have a compelling sense of purpose:** Very few start-up entrepreneurs have real focus. Why are you in business? What is your end goal? Then decide what your unique selling proposition (USP) is. What is different with your business compared to the competition? Then boil the USP down to just one line. This is your vehicle that is going to get you where you want to be. Make it clear, compelling and powerful. It will help you attract investors, partners, staff and customers.

Think creatively, says Paul

'The right team will pay dividends', says Paul. He continues:

Bill Nguyen, co-founder and CEO of Color Inc, successfully raised $41 million from the top venture capital firm in Silicon

Valley with a 45-minute verbal presentation and no business plan, but by effectively building a team of top engineers and marketers he was seen as a good investment because of his track record of launching and getting highly profitable exits for investors.

I recall Phillipa James, who had an excellent product called Breathing Relief, which eliminated snoring. She'd got lost in writing a business plan that halted the progress of her business. I suggested she focus on just producing a concise one-page exec summary that would get her meetings with angel investors and to put most of her energy on creating momentum in selling the product and building contacts. Her business has now successfully raised investment, and the product is stocked by Waitrose and independent chemists.

Dreams become reality

With the right clarity, customer awareness, courage, cooperation and creativity, dreams can become a reality. Dreams are free – they carry no price tag. When creativity is added, magic can happen on a very small price tag.

Whilst writing this book I was reminded of a simple business idea that had a major impact on the world. Berry Gordy, Jr, founder of Motown Records, had a vision. He borrowed $700 from family and friends and bought a small house that he called Hitsville USA. Inspired by the production methods of the Ford Motor Company in Detroit (dubbed Motor City) he adapted the car production line business model to set up and run his own record label producing a conveyor belt of hit records by attracting local artists with raw talent and an assembly line of young writers, musicians and producers. They were also creative in how they utilized the small space and in creating sounds. They were customer savvy; the company held weekly meetings, and staff and artists would listen to the songs up for release. They were simply asked: Would you buy the record or would you rather buy a sandwich? If a song didn't pass that simple test it wasn't released.

It was genius, and the spirit of cooperation and friendly competition between the differing songwriters and producers to create a hit record, and between the artists, led to one of the most successful and iconic record labels in music history. It launched the careers of some of the most significant artists in history, including Stevie Wonder, Michael Jackson and the Jackson 5, Marvin Gaye, Smokey Robinson and Diana Ross and the Supremes. The Motown story is not a perfect one; there were questions raised about whether the musicians and artists were fairly rewarded, but the remarkable achievement is unquestionable. What Berry Gordy did was intuitively to combine a good business model and some of the simple principles of resourcefulness covered in this book.

The question is: What business model might work for you? What do others do? Perhaps like Berry Gordy you need to think creatively and look to another industry to innovate in your own. What works in your business? What needs tweaking? Or are you going to need to create something new? The answers may take a while to answer, and things may need to change a few times, but your mindfulness of the question and your willingness to be flexible and creative will help you.

In the case of Foluke's online magazine and awards there are several options for the future business model: paid membership services and events; paid advertising; and providing business-to-business services for the magazine's large readership. Foluke started by surveying her readers on what they want and need to help get it right. If you're in a similar situation it pays to check in with yourself, your customers' needs, and skilled experts in your network.

What's going to work for you?

Now the question of creativity comes right back to you. By thinking creatively you can shape your business to progress. Here are a few examples of what other business owners have done and are doing, including a few of their tips.

Easy does it; then spread your wings to greater things

Rita Bailey is a friend and accomplished trainer and management consultant who has worked with leading companies such as Microsoft across the world. Creativity is something she's had to adopt personally and professionally to build her business, so I was keen to get her view on how she had used creativity to get to the top of her profession and to help senior managers to get the best out of themselves. Rita says of her career:

I was among the first wave of coaches in the UK, so the whole period was creative, like finding ways to clarify what coaching is and making it beneficial for people. I realized I wanted to work with the decision makers, the managers that made things happen, people that turned visions into reality, generating my ideas around how I wanted to create a business about leadership that also suited me and was truly creative. At times you can feel you are going against the grain. I endeavoured to stay freshly inspired every day and remaining curious in that way you are always coming up with new ways of thinking about developing your business.

Rita adds these tips and her own experience:

Being creative isn't a linear, familiar process. It can look quite random most of the time as we open up more to this process. It challenges us to open up to what is authentic. It requires us to trust ourselves and the process we are in. It also at times needs us to work with structure so that our ideas can come to fruition. Working as an independent consultant certainly brings up new challenges for me daily. How much time I spend on client work and how much time I spend on new ideas I want to create something new with. It's always important to allocate time on things that are important to you, what I call the 'slow burn' projects that you've had the idea for a while but maybe you get so busy delivering projects hardly finding the time. In my experience it's the dream stuff, the book, new service, research, speaking, building alliances, personal development. For me I'm now at a new stage wanting to create in new ways including embracing more time to write and speak. I am certainly looking forward to this part of the journey and the inspiration that comes with this. Give yourself the space to explore your ideas, what is important to you. Talk to friends, people in your networks; do some research; ensure you have up-to-date information: all will help to shape and give confirmation to your ideas.

Ingenious inventors and technology wizards

Jerome is a former head of IT who has worked at big City firms. After years of managing IT for others he decided to do his own thing. Jerome combined IT skills and creativity to develop a range of customer relationship, management and software tools. His main business product, Campus Interaction, allows schools and colleges to interact online amongst themselves and with selected audiences outside, such as potential employers for the university graduates. Together we developed a two-page business plan to map out his goals and actions for the years ahead. Jerome's business has already taken off with schools and colleges in India and is now looking to develop in the UK. His business is growing in staff and profit, and the challenge for Jerome now is becoming a visionary entrepreneur managing an ever growing team. He has shrewdly introduced a head of human resources to help him find the best talent to build the business and to free him up to focus on creatively building the business and new products and services.

Here's what Jerome says about his journey:

Creativity has played a big role in my business and its growth. Of course initially it was born out of my own skills with IT, computing, software development and customer relationship platforms. But I then needed to convert that into a clear, creative strategy for the business. This is when I met Rasheed through TiE UK and the British Library. But it's also been important to come up with creative solutions that customers actually want. Each project is different; what each school or college needs varies, so you have to be creative. Finally as my business grows in size, shape, structure and profits, these will all require creative solutions. We are a growing business, so I've had to find new offices – and I've also needed to be creative myself. I'm meeting new contacts and I'm facing new opportunities and challenges. The thrill has been applying my IT problem-solving skills to business.

Powering forward through partnerships and new products

Tum has built his internet marketing business using his creativity and through clarity, customers and cooperation. He says: 'As my business has begun to grow and succeed, one of the key lessons I've learnt has been the value of cooperation in my business.' He's been very creative in going one step further than many by developing new products and services *with* his like-minded clients, helping the businesses to grow and combining his internet marketing know-ledge and their excellent service. Tum says: 'Only when we get this dance right do both of us grow and prosper.'

Tum is world-travelled, and has an interest in tourism, sustainability and business. He's brought all his skills and passions together with his new venture, Here is Zambia.com, a website he hopes will become the leading resource for those visiting and living and work-ing in the country. He and I are also looking to create an online self-development resource combining my expertise and his ability to reach new audiences. To create such partnerships and products Tum refers to 'an almost unspoken agreement that implies responsibility on both parties to work together for our common good'. He adds: 'I'm always surprised that more businesses don't find other *complementary* businesses to cooperate with – an easy way for both of them to benefit by sharing their customers.'

Social media star

Savvy small businesses utilize social media. They realize that social media are a powerful way to punch beyond their weight. Social media can also work well hand in hand with the traditional marketing methods.

What media of communication are you most confident with? Perhaps you are an excellent writer and love sharing stories. Then perhaps writing a blog, articles and an e-book for your website and other online platforms could work for you. Foluke of *Precious Online* has recently created an online Precious community, forum and social media page to extend her dialogue with readers.

Jason the personal trainer is the classic example of a business owner for whom using video – including on his website – was a great move. Jason once told me that when potential clients have had a taster session and met him in person they were invariably keen to go ahead and book in training sessions. Likewise his self-defence workshops at schools are highly visible. Adding imagery and video of Jason working with people of all ages brought his business to life and helped convert business far more quickly. In the past it meant hours spent writing letters trying to explain to people what he does and convincing them of his service. This can now be done in minutes through seeing his personal training or schools workshops on video.

Expert express

The expert express is all about establishing yourself as a leader in your given field. This may be about developing a profile speaking at events, conferences and in the media or through writing.

The expert express is suited to people who are specialists with a proven track record who are good communicators. So my Harley Street weight loss doctor client is a brilliant example of someone whom the expert model would work well for. He is an expert (a medical doctor). He has a speciality (weight loss for women over a certain age). He has celebrity and wealthy clients. He is a great communicator in the spoken and written word. He has a warm personality and professional style. He also has the right face for TV and the right voice for radio. He has just written his first book, which has now become a best-seller. This is important, as his book will make him more appealing to places he may want to write and speak for. He is also now writing for a popular international journal, so he is well on his way. The task with him now is to explore whether he may be keen on radio or TV. He already does public speaking, and all this experience is making him far more open to doing more profile-raising work. It also helps that it ties in with the fact that he has something to say and genuinely cares.

The expert route will become increasingly crowded, so your integrity and professionalism and having something of real value to share and offer will be key. If you take this route, these are some pointers:

- ♥ Be clear on your goals.
- ♥ Identify the topics that you can speak and are passionate about.
- ♥ Work to your strengths (spoken, written, audio or visual media as appropriate).
- ♥ Know your stuff.
- ♥ Study the media or outlets that you're interested in.
- ♥ Network, network, network and become visible.
- ♥ Start small and build up: local paper, small informal lunchtime talk, e-book.
- ♥ See if it works for you and for others, and develop it from there.

Finally, you, your materials and all that you say and do must reflect what you say that you stand for. If you move into doing national media and television I recommend you have media training. Having a background in media and media training, I'd stress that once you have a high visibility it's important you are skilled and robust enough to handle it.

Be your own brand

For me the magic happens when, as I put it, you 'become who you are'. Becoming who you are is about embracing your own magic and being in the world. I run a workshop called Be Your Own Brand, which is all about building a business around you, utilizing the tools, techniques and methods that work for you. It looks at how you can raise your visibility, profile and profits on little or no PR budget, and is based on many of the things we have explored in this book. In my case my career as a coach was born out of my own 'Become who you are' approach and from using the media I know well: writing for newspapers and websites, appearing on radio and TV, and speaking and running workshops. My career has basically been a new creative expression of the skills I developed as a press officer, trainer and singer-songwriter and around my people skills as a coach and speaker. How can you use your own skills and talents more and use what you highlight as your unique approach? As we explored in Chapter 1, how can you use your unique story further to develop your brand and your business?

Framework and flexibility

We're almost back where we started in this chapter. Your success will rely on being continually creative to develop and navigate the challenges that will emerge. That will require a blend of strategic flexibility and framework – including utilizing the tools we've covered. Your goals for tomorrow ultimately are about what you do today, and within daily life it's easy to be sidetracked by day-to-day issues or indeed your creative plans, so the following tips will help.

Focus, fluid and free

♥ **Focus:** There will be times when you need to focus on one specific action – like serving a customer or meeting a deadline for a pitch. There'll be times that you need to address a key issue like raising your profits by an extra £1,500 a month. On these occasions, be absolutely clear on the action and the outcome required. In focus we are very conscious of what it is that we are doing and apply ourselves to it.

♥ **Fluid:** These are the times when you go with the flow. It means being mindful and addressing what is arising in your business day by day to move ahead: making customer calls, raising invoices and doing marketing. Think about middle-distance athletes. They are aware of the goal to win and of the pack, study the twists and turns of the race and run their own race, but adjust and respond as appropriate. They may have their own game plan but also can adapt. We need to be conscious of what we are doing but operate from a more relaxed mindfulness where we have a blend of intelligent action and intuitive feeling that guides us.

♥ **Free:** This is when we are lost in the moment. In fact it is a timeless state. In free mode we are at one with what is going on. Athletes often refer to this as 'being in the zone'. It can be like the powerful 'at oneness' that happens in meditation or that we may experience when we are on a stunning beach or lost in an experience before the mind kicks back in. The conscious mind is absent – it gets to take a break and relax. It's not something we often experience in business, as we focus overly on conscious aspects. However, it would seem that it's here – or somewhere between here and the fluid state – that some of the magical inspiration and creative ideas are born.

Profit, profile or pleasure

Being creative is great, but stay on track. Check the key activities you are doing:

1 **Profit:** Is this action leading to me being paid (adequately)?

2 **Profile:** Is the action raising my profile with appropriate audiences?

3 **Pleasure:** Is what I'm doing enjoyable, interesting, fun and rejuvenating?

The ideal is that everything should be all three. I actually believe that for the soul trader it should be at least two of the three.

Fun time, family time and free time

We started this chapter by exploring what you are like at your best, and to be at your best you need to know when to work and when to rest. It's also important to remember and recognize that lots of the energy, creativity and inspiration for your business will actually emerge from the times that you are resting, relaxing, recharging and reconnecting with your friends, family and pastimes.

When I worked with the top entertainment accountant who was doing great in business we spent time focusing on his personal, fun and family goals, and quite right too. Remember, we started this journey by getting clarity on what's important for you in your life – don't let it be an afterthought; ensure that fun and balance are things you build into every day:

- ♥ What are your personal, social and home priorities?
- ♥ What hobbies and pastimes do you want to spend time on and how much?
- ♥ What ways that work for you can you introduce to keep you in balance?

I've learnt that for many of my clients their own pastimes and interests actually bring a great deal of balance and creativity to their business. For me, quiet time is especially important, as I work with people week in and week out. A few years into my coaching career I rediscovered singing and recording – for my own pleasure. This time away from my coaching and speaking gives balance, distance and a different type of perspective and creativity, which I find refreshing when I return to my work.

SUMMARY

Soul traders recognize that being creative, flexible and imaginative is a key element of starting and growing a business and a key element in overcoming challenge, change and difficulties. They also realize that having fun and balance at home and at work are important aspects of enjoying the business journey.

1 Know what you're like at your best and play to your strengths.

2 Use your time and energy wisely and use tools and technology to support not distract.

3 Fresh ideas: learn when to air, park, introduce and change them.

4 Tailor the tools and techniques that give you the right framework and flexibility.

5 Write a two-page business plan – and take 10 minutes a week to review and update it.

6 Consider and shape the right business model for you; this may evolve over time.

7 Your daily actions will ultimately shape your outcomes and profitability.

COMPASSION

How to truly take care
of business

Love is the vocation, destination, liberation and medication.

If your heart isn't in it,
why are you?

Just as your body can't survive without your heart, you won't be able to live a fulfilled life as an entrepreneur – or as a human being – without compassion. If your heart isn't in your business it will become meaningless. If you're not compassionate toward yourself you'll stunt your own growth and progress. If you're not caring toward your customers and those in your life they'll leave you. You'll struggle to get out of bed in the morning and wonder why you're even doing what you are doing. You'll find that you are constantly battling yourself, customers, friends and family. You'll find yourself in a life and a business that you loathe rather than love.

I often meet business owners who have lost heart during the journey. Their light has gone out. Their belief in themselves has been extinguished. They are tough on themselves. They feel worthless. They're simply going through the motions. The love for what they do has gone – if they ever had it.

This chapter explores the power of compassion – connectedness, love and passion – and how it can transform and enrich your life, your business, those in your life and those whom your business serves.

What's love got to do with it?

The paradox about business is that it is often started because we wish to change our lives and those of the ones we love or because of a cause dear to our heart. But often within years or even months the love and the passion we had in the business has gone, as has our compassion for ourselves. One of the reasons is that – in the West in particular – the norm is that your value and worth are measured by *what you do* not *who you are*. They are based on what you accumulate (power, prestige, posts, possessions, people). It's one of the reasons the first question we ask someone is 'What do you do for a living?' It's why people feel that they're not good enough or that they won't be complete until they've achieved x, y or z. It's complete rubbish, but sadly it leads to seeing life through the lens of what's not in place, overlooking what *is* – your magic. It can result in business and everything else being reduced to something you do robotically rather than romantically, passionately and joyfully. When challenges arrive – small or large – this feeling of failure, self-doubt or not being good enough kicks in. This is a very loveless place to operate from. It can slowly or quickly erode your confidence, relationships and business.

Compassion – and its root, love – is the only cure for this empty feeling. I've coached many 'successful' people who still feel that they've not achieved and feel unfulfilled. Again this is all born of our false view that self-worth is based on what we gain and have rather than who we are (or even what we give and contribute).

Compassion is dear to my heart and led me into the work that I do today. I first really (re)discovered compassion during my time as a Samaritan volunteer. It was a transformational time for me. I'd left my full-time job and decided to follow my desire to become a singer. When I arrived for my shift as a Samaritan, for the first time in my life I felt I left myself – my ego – at the door. For those five hours I was present for someone who was at a point of difficulty in life. Singing was all about 'me, me, me'. Volunteering taught me to be empathetic to someone else. It enriched me in ways that words cannot describe. I wasn't trying to fix, solve or resolve. I was just being present, listening and empathetic. It brought a calming and soothing benefit – for both parties. I learnt about the human condition because I was open and listening for the first time.

This, combined with meeting so many singers who struggled with confidence and career–life balance, led me to retrain as a coach. As I went through this personal, career and – you might say – spiritual change I realized compassion is something that works both ways. I became compassionate to myself. This helped shape my 'Become who you are' approach as a coach, which is essentially about letting go of who you think you should be and discovering who you actually are – embracing yourself and life as it is. Essentially this is how I help all my clients, be it in business, corporate or public life.

For the soul trader compassion is especially important. You run your business because you care. Whether it's about making a difference in your own life or the lives of others, you care. Unless you care about yourself then you are living a lie or treating yourself as a second-class citizen.

I vividly remember working with a very intelligent, serious business owner whose clients included directors and major firms. Our first session was very strategic, yet we hadn't bonded or made headway. Then halfway through our second session he told me why he really wanted his business to succeed: to build schools in disadvantaged areas of the world. His whole demeanour changed; a warmth and gentleness in him changed the energy in the room, and we instantly found the momentum to advance his goals from a more powerful place of compassion.

So love actually has a lot to do with it. Soul traders want to run a business they love. They want to do things that they love. They wish to support their loved ones. They wish to run businesses in a caring and considerate manner.

Ask yourself these questions and answer them honestly:

- ♥ Are you kind and compassionate to yourself or tough on yourself?
- ♥ Are you considerate and thoughtful when it comes to those in your life and business?
- ♥ What would the benefits be of operating and speaking more from compassion?

FIGURE 7.1   Compassion in all areas of your life

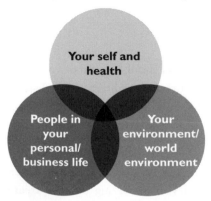

Rasheed oqunlaru © 2011

Love you, love what you do and love others too

Many people who attend my talks (and people I work with individually) are surprised when I tell them directly 'Whether you pursue your goals or not is immaterial; your value comes from who you already are today, not what you might achieve tomorrow.' I've told millionaires and those who barely have a penny. People are surprised to hear it, because we're programmed endlessly to 'do' and 'improve'. They're surprised because I'm a coach and they expect me to focus on their goals and their tomorrows. But goals and tomorrows are nothing without an appreciation of yourself and what gifts you have today. It's this realization that can transform life from ordinary into extraordinary. It's almost like hearing a foreign language at first, but yet it resounds deeply at your core.

Nothing in life has any value unless you appreciate it. This begins with you. In fact, the word 'appreciate' means two things. First it means 'notice', 'acknowledge' or 'be aware of'. Its second meaning is 'grow in value over time', so when you appreciate in one sense you appreciate in the other; when you notice and value something or someone then it grows and develops. This starts with you.

1 **Love you:** Embrace who you are right now. See and value what's already in place. Focus on your strengths and talents. Yesterday is dead. Tomorrow is yet unborn. Happiness is the acceptance of who you are and what you are. Unhappiness is hankering after what you had or feel you lack. If this is an area that you struggle with, revisit the exercises in Chapters 1 ('Clarity') and 3 ('Courage'); they'll help reflect what you are back to you.

2 **Love what you do:** If you don't love what you do, stop now and find what you do. If you don't love the way that you're doing what you do, start doing it in a loving manner. There is that saying that home cooking is so special because it's 'made with love'. Perhaps putting your heart into what you do is the only missing ingredient.

3 **Love others too:** The moment you embrace yourself, you can embrace others. Care about those in your life and your business. Always be mindful, as we discovered in the earlier chapters, that they too have fears, ideas and concerns. Remembering this will make you empathetic to them.

I remember coaching a woman who'd been divorced by a rich businessman. There she was: a beautiful woman in a big, beautiful house. She'd been isolated from the family. She was wondering how to pick up the pieces of her life and what to do next. Before getting married she'd planned to set up her own shop. She now certainly had the money to do it. However, she felt worthless. She was blind to all the beauty she had within as a human being and to her skills and talents. She'd lost that insight somewhere during her marriage. I had to help her first to be compassionate toward herself and find kindness, which would mean that she'd value herself, be able to look at herself in the mirror, feel confident and begin to move forward.

Once compassion for oneself is in place, true self-confidence (re) emerges, the kind that can't be broken by anybody else 'falling out of love' with us.

Take care of you; take care of business

There are two dynamics to this. Are you taking enough care of yourself? And are you being empathetic and considerate toward everyone in your life and your business?

Jessica Huie is founder of Colorblind Cards and her own self-named PR company. We first met at the Precious Awards, where she won both Best Business and Entrepreneur of the Year – not bad at just 27 and balancing two businesses with being a single parent. Jessica says: 'I was driven by a desire to put ethnic diversity into the card market and ensure children had access to images which reflect their identity regardless of their race. I also recognized a gap in the market for a brand like Colorblind and was driven to pursue it.'

Despite the awards, a regular magazine column, celebrity clients and having greeting cards in high street stores, Jessica didn't think that she'd achieved much in business yet. Ambition and contribution are great qualities, but I sensed she needed compassion for herself for the next stage of progressing her career, so instead of being overly goal oriented we focused on putting time in for herself, exercise, yoga and meditation. Jessica has continued to build her business. Her card business is taking off overseas, and her more relaxed approach to her PR business serves her better.

Jessica says:

> My ambition hasn't dissipated as I've got older, but certainly my reasons for wanting to achieve have altered. I no longer place the same level of attachment on career success, as it's not my identity. One of the most important lessons I have learnt through experience, age and working with Rasheed is that I am not the awards on my mantle or the figure in my bank account. My self-esteem isn't pegged to my profile, and so any business decision I choose to make comes from a much healthier place. Compassion is caring, kindness and empathy. Compassion is a quality I seek to display in all areas of my life. It's important to care!

Jessica adds: 'The biggest joys come from developing as a human being, and the irony of life is that the more you focus on being the best human being you can be, the commercial and superficial aspects fall graciously and easily into place.' These words have rung true. A new relationship, wedding bells and a new baby all followed. I'm not sure that these kinds of things can really emerge without first loving the one within.

Rasheed's 12 tips for personal growth

1 Take responsibility for your life and actions (let others do the same).

2 Adopt an attitude of acceptance and appreciation of yourself and others.

3 Create space, support and simplicity in all areas of your life.

4 Develop rich relationships and let go of draining ones.

5 Take care of your 'self', your health and then your wealth.

6 Goals: plan, prepare, visualize, pursue and review, but be flexible – life changes.

7 Break big tasks into small steps and work from your strengths and others'.

8 Avoid conflict; choose compassion and cooperation.

9 Adopt nourishing words and action: 70 per cent of the messages we give and receive daily are negative – make yours 'nutritious'.

10 Use both head and heart: use your intelligence *and* trust your instincts.

11 Know when to work and rest; do what you do best; let others do the rest.

12 Embrace life: flowers grow through sun and rain – both are needed.

Are you losing sleep?

Many entrepreneurs lose too much sleep. Your sleep will be one of the signs of whether you are in balance with yourself. It is a good indicator of whether you are in tune with what's dear to you. It will tell you if you are working too hard or well enough. It will tell you if you're being kind to yourself or not. It will disturb you if you are too tough on others.

For me my starting point is my downtime, rest time and sleep. Without these things I can't serve others. It's a powerful creative time when most of my ideas emerge. There's a powerful link between this chapter and the preceding one ('Creativity'). Sleep plays many vital roles. It is essential to our survival and for reconnecting to ourselves. It's where the conscious falls back into the unconscious. It's where the body repairs. It's where dreams and ideas emerge. If you're losing sleep you're losing your creative essence.

Sleep easy – watch for the signs

- ♥ Working too hard (long hours, stress, irritability)? You need to ease off.
- ♥ Can't switch off? Take a break (the more wound up you are, the more unwinding time you need).
- ♥ Tough on yourself or cold with others? Be kinder and warmer as necessary.
- ♥ Don't trust yourself enough? You need to use your heart as well as your head.
- ♥ Listen to your body – it will tell you when to work or rest and when to play or create.

**RELAX AND RECENTRE:
10 MINUTES' SILENCE EACH DAY**

Busy life? Busy mind? Taking as little as 10 minutes each day to sit silently can have a profound effect on helping you recentre and reduce stress. Try it. I've produced a free 10-minute relaxation meditation that you can listen to or download from my website (**www.rasaru.com**) or watch on my YouTube channel (**www.youtube.com/ogunlaru**).

Rasheed's seven work–life balance tips

Being compassionate and effective starts with your work–life balance and well-being.

At home

1 Have a home spring clean to calm, focus and improve your daily life.

2 Eat a balanced diet, sleep well and exercise; it boosts energy and cuts stress.

3 Give time and attention to key relationships.

4 Set five specific personal priorities for your life and focus on them.

5 Give all you haven't used for over six months to friends or charity – it relieves you, helps others and allows space for new opportunities.

6 Take time out – give yourself half an hour alone to relax or focus on your life. Set time aside for loved ones.

7 Cut TV and internet time by an hour and give it to you or to loved ones.

At work

1 Carve out 10 minutes daily and weekly to plan and review your business.

2 Schedule time in your diary for your family, friends, fun, interests and holidays.

3 Start and end the day with a clear desk to reduce stress.

4 Have a desk and file clear-out monthly: it can keep your mind clear and relaxed.

5 Deal with key tasks first; handle calls and e-mails at set times, warmly and concisely.

6 Arrive and leave on time. It sounds simple – make it a habit. If you work alone or find it tough then set an alarm so that you do it.

7 Go out of your office (or home office) at lunch to ensure you take breaks, and use technology to support and simplify your working life not to rule or complicate it.

Compassionate courage

As we've touched on there may be major personal and professional challenges as you develop your business. Your business may take off; it may hit the rocks. How will you respond within yourself and with others if things get rough? How will you respond if the economy slides or if major problems emerge with customers or suppliers? These things will require not just courage to press ahead but the kindness and consideration toward yourself and others to resolve them and move forward.

It is compassionate courage that Rachel found and applied. She had built a business empire, made millions and become a recognizable face: all the things that most business owners dream of. But a series of events that she discusses in her book *Business Nightmares* meant that it was all lost. During the coaching session that I touched on in Chapter 3 ('Courage') I asked what she wanted to do next. She said she wanted to make a target goal of £10 million and then she'd study under all the great teachers, gather their wisdom and put it together in a way others would understand. I asked 'Why don't you do that now?' It was a conversation that transcended business; we discussed life, purpose and contribution. It was a compassionate conversation.

Sure enough, as we spoke more, Rachel revealed that she was on what many might call a self-discovery and spiritual journey – and that she wanted to bring this more compassionate and feminine energy to the business world. What's more, she told me about the book that she was just finishing writing called *Business Magic*, which is all about the subtler side of business and what emerges when we operate from a more compassionate and intuitive space.

In some ways I never really coach anybody about business. I ask questions that get to the heart of who they are. I invite people to reconnect to their heart and create their business from this space. It actually requires a huge amount of compassion to operate from this space, but it enables real transformation.

Are you willing to be compassionate enough to let go of how you think you should be and to live your life and run your business from who you truly are?

Building your business from the heart

Sometimes your mind can hold you back, and your mind and your heart can move you forward. I first met Donald the surveyor on a TV training course I was running. He got back in touch after watching a video of mine on my YouTube channel called 'Is your mind in a riot?' He recognized he had a noisy mind overly caught up with the past and with future worries, which was holding him back personally and in business. Instead of starting with business we focused on calming the mind and got him working from his heart. Donald says:

> I asked Rasheed what he meant by compassion. I've always associated it with sympathy and for a need to alleviate mental or physical pain in others. What I've learnt is that we can extend this to ourselves instead of the unkindness that is often there. If I saw anyone treating another with the cruelty that I have subjected myself to it would make me very angry.

Within weeks he was becoming kinder to himself. He adopted a more relaxed and compassionate approach to supporting his son, who was going through difficulty. Donald adds:

> I'm only at the beginning of this journey. I still wake up some mornings with intense negative thoughts and feelings. It's a battle I've been fighting all my adult life. However, things are improving in a sustainable way. We must follow our dreams and to do that we need to allow ourselves to have dreams as opposed to fantasies. Freeing yourself from self-destructive tendencies is critical, and the first step is compassion.

He's now pouring this approach into his business, addressing goals he's had in his *head* for years, now that he's following his *heart*, including improvements to his systems and website, broadening his network and giving talks.

Sweet dreams

Compassion and kindness are hallmarks of Hom, founder of a growing tea company. Hom was already a successful entrepreneur when we met at a business growth seminar I was running. Ethical and humanitarian issues have always been dear to his heart. Born in Nepal into a large family of modest means, he eventually founded *Society* magazine highlighting social and ethical matters. When the publishing industry fell on tough times he asked himself what to do next. He knew it had to be grounded, rooted, and related to the planet. Then, in a dream, it appeared to him: tea. He had literally dreamt of setting up a tea business. He started learning everything about tea, but contribution had to play a part; he wanted to create jobs and opportunities in Nepal, a beautiful part of the world with much poverty, and so he set up the Anglo-Himalayan Tea Company bringing Nepalese tea to the UK, one of the world's biggest tea-drinking nations. He is also working to develop a 'Tea Park' in Nepal to help showcase the country's teas to the world and further boost employment. He is putting his years of business and publishing to good effect engaging with celebrities and politicians to bring awareness of Nepalese issues.

Hom's business is taking off; his teas are stocked by several suppliers, in Harrods and in several restaurants, much of it achieved through Hom's warm, personal charisma. I called him as I wrote this chapter to tell him that I planned to mention him. He told me he'd just left hospital following a mild heart scare. Fortunately it was nothing other than stress. He recognized it as a sharp reminder that compassion must operate in all directions – within oneself and outwardly in your world.

Hom is operating in a space where many soul traders are starting to: where the economical, social, environmental, spiritual and political issues all melt together into simply running businesses that are of value to the wider world. He says:

> *To me business is not just about making money. It is about service, joy, happiness. I went into the tea business because I wanted to set up a business that was part of people's lives. Drinking tea is at the heart of many cultures. It brings families and friends together. It is also about making a difference to the lives of the people from the part of the world that I am from.*

Working from your heart

Lewis set up his business, Get Work Experience.com, based on an issue close to his heart. He saw a growing problem of talented graduates who couldn't get work and lots of small businesses needing good-calibre people to grow, so he decided to set up a business to solve both problems. Lewis recalls:

> *The start of the recession led to a number of my friends, as office juniors, being made redundant. These were talented individuals who were being denied an opportunity to make a real impact in their industry due to the economic conditions. In addition, many small and medium-sized enterprises could see their opportunities to grow in the downturn but were unable to compete effectively as they didn't have access to the calibre of talent their larger competitors held. As a result of this clear disparity, and passionate about my own ability as a young professional, I resigned from my job to launch Get Work Experience.*

As he puts it, 'Simply, it is a "win–win" situation'; graduates get work experience and longer internships that hopefully lead to a full-time job at the end of the line, and businesses are saved time and money by getting good-calibre, graduate-level talent. It solves a business problem, social problem and economic problem at a time of record unemployment amongst under-25-year-olds and when businesses are crying out for talent and need to be creative and resourceful.

Lewis is a true soul trader. He genuinely cares about his work and those he serves. He has integrated his passion, his business and his skills with issues that he cares about, and is making a contribution. When you do this, life, work and your values are aligned. Lewis is pleased:

> *My biggest achievement is our work promoting the value of young people that has led to the placing of students and graduates with companies ranging from one-man bands to large international corporations, with over 78 per cent of*

placements extending beyond the initial typical three-month
internship period. For me, compassion has played a big part
in our success; dealing with people and their individual
personal situations demands it! Passion is the other vital
ingredient; to get a business off the ground, that passion
enables you to put the hours in and deal with the ups and
downs!

Lewis works long hours, but after attending my Your Life, Your Business workshop at the British Library he took action on his work–life balance; as he puts it, he separates time on his business from time with his friends, family and fiancée.

The win of working from the heart is that you enjoy every minute and feel better and more motivated. You also win more business, because people want to do business with you. People refer other people to you without you asking for it. Lewis hopes that others will set up businesses that emerge from issues that they care about. 'My advice would be to find how your business can extend from your passions. If you do, you'll make an impact.'

Compassion is contagious

If you care about other people they begin to care about you. The opposite is also true: if you don't care about other people, sooner or later people will see through you and stop buying from or into you.

For some reason in life our default is simply to give what we get. We don't go that extra mile. We don't initiate that slight change that can transform someone's day. We tend to be safe and be the same as everyone else, so if nobody else smiles on the street we don't. But every now and then we break out of the box: we'll smile in the street or we'll stop and give someone a hand. We'll call someone out of the blue to ask how they are doing. We'll offer to give someone a little help with something they are not good at. Suddenly the dynamic has changed. Suddenly our mundane life has been lifted by the act of kindness, and we see it in the recipient, who thanks us – with genuine thanks. For the person you have helped, it has been a 'day changer'. You begin to shift business and life from the transactional to the transformational.

Walk into the business networking event with the intention of helping others. Take a moment to help another business owner and friend. Call a long-time customer or supplier and offer a free product or extra session. Give a concession to someone who's genuinely in need. If you do this genuinely, with real attention to the person you are helping, something shifts within that person, who recognizes that, yes, you may be running a business and may be selling something, but you really care. You change the relationship; you are no longer a service provider or a stranger but a valued contact or business that is part of the person's life. It is powerful.

Being compassionate becomes contagious. You find that people react warmly to you as a default. You find that those people themselves often begin to warm to themselves and others. There are many opportunities I've gained not because I'm the only one who could do the job but because I'm the one who is easy to work with, understands, and is compassionate to the client group.

During writing this book I noticed that knock-on effect. I put a few of my contacts in touch, sparking more conversations and cooperation. One person directs another to a useful group, and someone hires another to do a piece of work, and all parties extend their networks. All this is done courteously, because all parties genuinely want to help one another.

TIP   How are you treating life? Many people tell me that life and others are giving them a hard time. But what's your relationship to life? Are you the first to beat yourself up? Be on your side. Once you embrace life you become one with it. It stops being you against the world. Once you see that events in life are happening – rather than happening to you – everything suddenly transforms.

Try a little tenderness

The invitation to the soul trader is to be compassionate and consistent. Compassion isn't something to be compartmentalized; it's not that you care for others and neglect yourself, or treat some customers or suppliers kindly and are harsh with those who are difficult or whom you don't like. Life and business will become stunted and unsustainable that way.

In recent times an interesting shift has occurred among many high-profile entrepreneurs. Whilst many successful entrepreneurs have always – quietly or publicly – been involved in philanthropy, charities and causes, many are now asking themselves deep questions about creating and accumulating wealth – many utilizing their wealth to help enrich the world in which they live. Oprah Winfrey, renowned for her generosity, supports several social causes and issues to raise human consciousness, and built a school in South Africa. Warren Buffett, once the world's richest man, gave over $37 billion to the charitable foundation of Bill Gates and Melinda Gates. They, in turn, have been increasingly involved in their foundation to fight disease and promote education – particularly in developing countries. In fact Bill Gates reportedly gave up the day-to-day running of Microsoft to focus on the work of the foundation.

Whether this increase of giving is altruistic, conscience-clearing or the result of a more aware consciousness, there seems to be a real awareness that this question of what we contribute, what we can do and what we can give back is pronounced.

Tenderness will take different forms and degrees based on where you are at. It can be as little as a kind word. It may be about that £5 a month donation to a cause. It may take a far more structured and extensive form. You will have differing means, concerns and circumstances to the next person. Being mindful is the start and can help throughout.

Leadership from the heart

Tomorrow's leaders will not lead dictating from the front,
or directing from the back, but from the centre, led by the heart.

We've all seen organizations and businesses that have been led poorly and uncompassionately. How will you choose to lead? How will you work with, manage and engage with those who work for and with you and who buy from you?

Pippa is a chairman and chief executive working across the health and homelessness sectors. She has always played a caring role throughout her life, including as a registered nurse, through her work and with her family. When we met it was clear that she needed to devote some of that care and attention to herself. She's now doing that so she can sustainably carry on with her work as a leader.

Pippa's rich knowledge of practitioner and strategic expertise, combined with her compassionate style, makes her a modern leader from the heart. Pippa has a practical view on compassion and leadership:

> *Compassion is simply about respect and a sense of trust in others. Throughout life we have encounters with people, whether transitory or more permanent. Having worked with people in desperate need, to those at higher levels trying to solve society's challenges, I believe that everyone has a contribution to make. Compassion is about valuing the best in everyone. A good leader is someone who understands an ideal, and then takes people on a journey of pursuit. Of course, this must be within a governance and business structure, but the art is to enable people to effect and own the desired outcomes. Even better leadership is supporting those who need to make a change for themselves.*

Francis is chief executive of a charity. We met at a conference soon after his appointment to the position, and he approached me for coaching for his new role. He wasn't interested in the old command-and-control leadership. He introduced a collaborative, compassionate style. Despite the challenges of reduced funding and having to cut staff numbers he has been creative and compassionate. This refreshing style is beginning to have an impact with his peers in his sector through his honest, open approach – leading to collaborations. His long-term vision includes being more involved in helping address issues in Sierra Leone, which he told me has one of the lowest incomes per capita in the world. I wouldn't be surprised if he does in time.

Francis and Pippa are examples of the leadership from the heart that I am beginning to see and that we need in business and organizations.

As a business owner, you are a leader. Do you realize the power and influence that you have in your own business world and in your wider world? What will be the impact if you run your business from this space of compassionate leadership?

Put your heart into everything you do

Stop for a moment. Think a little about where you are right now in life and business. What are your circumstances? How does compassion relate to you? Are there a few more conversations you need to have with family members? Do you need to let any members of your team know how much you appreciate them? Do you need to take more care of yourself? What are the hours that you're working at the moment? Do they need to be reduced? Could you put in a regular holiday? I invite you to put in the holiday now. Put in the 'you' time now.

Life is something that you cannot put off until tomorrow, tomorrow and tomorrow. I've worked with many business owners who also have good social causes that they want to support when they build up their business. In what way could you do that now?

SUMMARY

Soul traders come to realize that compassion is what brings real fulfilment and quality to all their personal and business relationships. They realize it is what brings real quality to their lives and can be used to create products, services, teams and businesses. They realize it is a means by which they can have impact and contribute to the world in which they operate in a small or large way – and often both.

1 Take care of your health, yourself and then your wealth.

2 Ensure that you love you, what you do and those whom you serve.

3 Sustainability: take time out to reward, re-energize and nourish yourself and the business.

4 Find the compassionate courage to follow your own path in business.

5 Find ways to support the issues that you really care about.

6 Lead your business from the heart not from your head.

7 Embody your values and carry out your day-to-day business with care.

CHANGE

How to face, shape and embrace it

It is not the strongest of the species that survives,
nor the most intelligent, but the one most responsive to change.
(CHARLES DARWIN)

So we've been on a journey looking at you, your business, who you are, where you're at, what you want, where you want to get to and your key steps to move forward. You've also clarified what your customers, contacts, suppliers and other key players in your life want and have greater insight into how they view the world. We've also brought these things together, lifting the lid of business to get to the heart of it to create a dynamic business you're passionate about and your customers love. We've seen that the key to all of this is relationships.

This closing chapter of the book covers change – the 'constant' throughout your business journey. We'll look at facing it, explore if you can shape it, and learn to embrace it. Change is especially significant in business. It's one of the areas of life where change often arrives first and most profoundly. The start of the 21st century has been a time of considerable change in the global, business, technological, political, social and ethical landscape, so it's important that you're mindful of this, how it affects you and your business and how it is that you can move with this change.

All change

The nature of life is change. It can be frustrating, frightening and unsettling, but it's important for you to remember that you are a part of it. You're an aspect of change. No two days are the same. You've changed from birth, through infancy and adolescence and into maturity, and it never stops. Your body has changed. You've changed your mind about things. Your feelings change regularly. You've changed jobs. Maybe you've changed your business as well. This is the nature of life.

Interestingly we have a dualistic relationship to change. On the one hand there are many changes we want: more customers, new relationships and more money. On the other hand there are certain changes we don't want – we want some things to stay the same. As we wrap things up we'll look at moving forward with a more rounded way to help you and your business. And guess what? In business we're often the cause of change – entrepreneurs invent and innovate. You're driving the change!

When I began my career at the age of 18 the business world looked completely different. I had a typewriter on my desk, and we shared one computer and a huge printer in the office. There was no internet, no social media. Few people had mobiles or cell phones.

Information passed through written memos and by post. People still sent telex messages! Now people are using handheld devices and tablets, and no doubt all of these things will change. The technology *will* change. The one thing we know about life is change.

The birth of the internet, which really began in the 1990s as far as the public and business were concerned, was a sea change moment. Few if any recognized the degree it would change business, our world and our day-to-day lives. It was the moment business changed. Some sensed it; some ignored it. Some businesses embraced it, and others buried their heads in the sand. Entire industries, such as the major music labels, were slow to respond and suffered hugely. Meanwhile other companies embraced the change. Apple took the lead in the new technologies and eventually won a large share of the potential spoils of record labels when they developed iTunes.

The internet changed the way we buy and sell products. Advertising and marketing were no longer the preserve of those that had the cash to promote their services on TV and radio and in the press. The internet meant that small businesses, as well as big businesses, had a window to the world.

Amazon is a very good example of a business that started small and has changed and developed in a way that remains true to itself. Amazon was one of the first names to emerge in the internet age. Back then this small business had an idea and utilized the new medium, the internet. Amazon built a business around selling books – and later CDs, DVDs and other products – online. Their name became synonymous with being one of the first places you'd look for any book. Years later when electronic tablets were developed and it became clear that publications could be provided and read on electronic devices, Amazon made the smart move to produce their own, the Kindle. This was a smart move of adapting to the times and leading rather than waiting. They spotted a change and moved with it. Increasingly soul traders will emerge and adjust in a similar way by flowing with change.

Sometimes change is profound. In recent years business has seen major change. Some of the world's biggest economies have run into major financial problems. Meanwhile emerging ones including Brazil, Russia, India and China have changed the 'game' – the speed of the change has astounded many. When you combine the growth of new economies and of internet business, one notable change is that a small one-person business can generate business all around the world. The first person to download my coach-yourself video was someone from the United States I've never met, who may have stumbled upon the product by surfing online.

Change can happen in the blink of an eye, and sometimes an external, economic or environmental change – or even a global one – can have a radical effect on your local business. The year I started writing this book, Japan, one of the world's biggest economies, suffered some major environmental challenges. They knocked the economy and swept away many businesses overnight. One day you have a business; the next you don't. Thankfully such events are rare, but they happen. It may be a more common but nonetheless devastating change that hits you – a leak in the office, a crash in your IT service, or your main client going bust. Last year my longest-running client closed, and so went thousands of pounds of my business.

There may well be major life changes. There may well be ill-health, pensions to consider, or bereavements. As we've explored, compassion will be necessary. All the goals and plans will be of limited use then – clarity, courage and compassion will be essential in such times.

Facing, embracing and shaping change

Some things you can't do anything about without doing huge detriment to yourself – like the physiological changes of the body. Likewise environmental, economic, global factors may be outside your direct control. Many of these are cyclical, and this book has been written during an economic slump. Other changes are likely to

FIGURE 8.1   From concern to influence

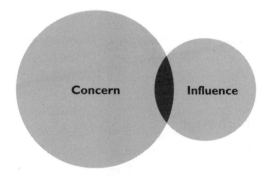

happen, so it's often wise to embrace them. As we've evolved as a species, one thing that hasn't stopped has been the development of technology. Many things have changed and can change: your career, your business, your product range and so on. Your mindset and your belief system will also play a part in this.

Figure 8.1 highlights the things that you are concerned about, whether they are worldly issues like the environment or everyday issues such as your health. Notice the intersection between concern and influence, where you can influence things in your life and the wider environment. Many people get 'lost' in their concern and forget their influence. Lewis's business addresses this; concerned about high youth unemployment, he looked at what he could influence and built his business around it. Suddenly his circle of influence became bigger.

Facing change

What changes have you seen in your life so far? What happened when you faced those changes? What changes are going on for you at the moment?

- ♥ Personally and in your health?
- ♥ At home?
- ♥ With friends and family?
- ♥ At work or in business?

♥ In your sector?

♥ In your broader environment?

What changes may arise in these areas? What are the changes that you can influence, starting with yourself? Merely gently asking and being aware of these questions may be very useful.

Embracing change

Change will happen. Be mindful of it – and even embrace the fact that you do or you don't like change. How are your customers' needs and circumstances changing? Speak to them. This will help you to be best placed to respond. Maybe the things that you want from life and business have changed during the time you've been reading this book. Goals are good to have but not necessarily to hold too fast to.

Accept that customers may well change. In fact, if the connection is rich, when the world changes your service or product may be a comfort that customers wish to hold fast to.

Shaping change

Soul traders can shape change. Anita Roddick put it this way: 'If you think you're too small to have an impact, try going to bed with a mosquito.' That quote proved apt. When Anita started the Body Shop from humble beginnings and a tiny shop, with big dreams to produce 'kind' cosmetics and toiletries on environmentally friendly, non-animal-tested, fair trade principles, many thought she'd make little impact. Anita and entrepreneurs like her changed the way that business and organizations operate. Eco-friendly, energy-efficient, sustainable business and fair trade are things we now expect most businesses to be aware of and address. That sea change happened in the course of a generation.

It was Gandhi who said 'Be the change you want to see in the world.' And he was a great example of a 'mosquito' – a humble and wise individual who changed the course of history. He began a move to independence, and proved that non-violence can change the way nation states behave, as well as moral and political and ethical landscapes.

Having been a young single parent and faced many challenges, Sabrina set up the Mobile Single Parents Project to support and inspire others in the same situation. She did so with virtually no money by sheer force of passion. In her own small way she is being the change – now. She is not waiting for some ideal moment. Her life still has challenges, but she is undeterred and meets everyone with warmth and compassion. That fortitude is a hallmark of a soul trader. They do what they do because it springs from their heart and because it needs to be done. Who knows the impact Sabrina has made on the lives of each and every one of the single parents she's worked with and the ripple effect?

Perhaps you might be the one to change your industry. Perhaps your approach in your industry may be unique.

Awareness, acceptance and appreciation

Change can be welcome or can be overdue, or it can arouse fear, anger and non-acceptance. I sometimes use Figure 8.2 when I'm giving talks or working with organizations facing change. As shown in Figure 8.2, by being aware and alert you can best anticipate. Then the emotions anger and acceptance will emerge: both have a place, but ultimately acceptance will be key to moving forward. By accepting you can take action, gather the resources, support or information you need, and adapt.

♥ **Awareness:** Many animals are wonderful at this. Be present, gently alert, and mindful of your environment. This may simply be about spending less time looking down at your desk and more looking at your business, customers, industry and economic environment. It may be about time at key events, engaging with customers and tuning in to industry

FIGURE 8.2   Surviving and thriving through change

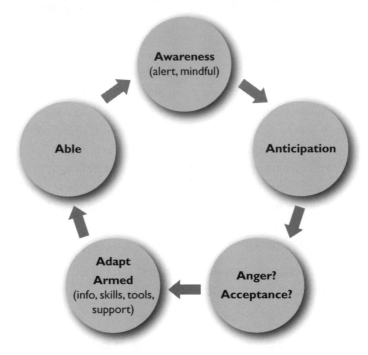

developments. It may be about listening and noticing changes in how your partner and loved ones are getting on.

- ♥ **Acceptance:** We come and we go. So do the seasons. Farmers do not seek to change them; they learn, accept and prepare for them. Acceptance is not about being passive. It is about embracing. Acceptance can spark change or the realization that you and your business should go your separate ways – if so, always do so with a good heart.

- ♥ **Appreciation:** The growth and enrichment that are gained from awareness are about acceptance: This is me. This is the world. This is how things are unfolding. As we become aware and accepting, we are able to see the beauty and purpose in all the seasons – not just spring and summer. As we explored in Chapter 7 ('Compassion'), it means two things: first noticing and valuing; then blossoming in value.

Where's the flow going?

As you move forward in your life and business, if you encounter hurdles and problems it's worth stopping, stepping back and looking at what's going on. If going against the flow isn't working for you, try going with it.

It was Einstein who commented that in the middle of change, difficulty and adversity there is opportunity. In my career it was the difficult times including redundancy and being pushed out of another job that were the making of me. They made me understand the working world and look at what I really wanted.

Where's the flow going?

- ♥ In business?
- ♥ With customers and competition?
- ♥ With technology and developments?
- ♥ Economically, socially, environmentally and politically?

This question is also an internal question:

- ♥ What's going on for you in your life?
- ♥ Are your priorities changing?
- ♥ Have your needs changed?
- ♥ Do you want things to change in your personal life?
- ♥ Do things need to change in your business?

These are important questions. Do not run from them. In the same way a severe pain within your body alerts you to health issues to address, constant worries that 'things aren't right' are telling you that things need to change.

In my case, watching where the flow is going has sometimes led me in a different direction, personally and professionally, to others, and it has made me distinct in my life and my work.

After doing well financially from his engineering business, Paul decided to focus on family life and to explore new horizons. Hom's health scare woke him up to the importance of going with his own flow and well-being. He says: 'I can see how businesses fail when people don't listen to their heart or when business is not done from the heart.'

Change your perspective

Our common view on change is that it comes along every now and then, and major change may come along every few months or years. But, as we touched on, it's happening all the time, *every* moment of every day for every day of your life. Cells of the body are dying and being born. Thoughts and feelings are emerging every few moments. Perhaps you have children or relatives who you notice seem to be growing every day and maturing every day. Change is not something that happens just to you. It happens through you. You are a manifestation of change, and change is manifesting itself in you.

When you see business through this lens you can be part of it – you are of that change. You become more attuned to every little thing that's going on in your business and far better placed to react, respond or accept as appropriate.

Making changes

A small business can adapt more swiftly than a large business. This may well account for many of the success stories of recent times such as YouTube having been so successful so quickly. It's a bit like the difference between a speed boat and a tanker. The speed boat is fast and can change direction quickly, while the tanker takes time to turn. Tankers may have the advantages of strength, size and resources, but the bulk and bureaucracy involved often slow things down. This is your advantage.

Pippa the chief executive has seen much personal change and steered organizations through it:

*Change is about embracing opportunity and using knowledge.
For me, this has been a combination of learning from people
and using travel adventures to broaden my horizons. Change
challenges security and exposes vulnerability, but in the
right environment this can be liberating, even exhilarating.
And lastly, we have an energy which is free and can be
directed in any direction we choose – let's make that a positive
resource.*

My business is constantly subtly changing: my focus, clients, projects and products. Over the years the shift in my work to fulfilment rather than success alone has been one that has served me, my profile and my clients. At first I was nervous about it. I was concerned my 'Become who you are' approach was too abstract or spiritual – especially for corporate clients – but I gradually embraced and integrated it. It was what made my service unique to me and relevant to the kind of customers I have.

Are there shifts and changes you can make or embrace?

Take the rough with the smooth

Years ago, ahead of pursuing singing, I remember hearing a song by Shara Nelson called 'Rough with the smooth'. In it she sang the lines: 'I no longer yearn for better times, I no longer yearn for better times, I no longer yearn for better times... I'll take the rough with the smooth and I wouldn't change a thing.' I was instantly arrested by the sentiment, and in the video she really seemed to mean it. She'd arrived at a realization that embracing life could be trans-formational. I wondered how someone could arrive at that place of being so accepting of the ups and downs of life.

I've learnt that only one thing separates those we call wise and those we dub foolish. The wise embrace life, and the foolish fight it. That's the only difference; the wise embrace life, themselves, all of it, with all its ups and downs. They don't negate what's going on or their own feelings, doubts and fears. The foolish are foolish only because they are negating who they are and what's going on.

The absence of content

You cannot grow unless you give yourself space. Space will help you identify and adjust to change. It's why we started in Chapter 1 with clarity. Having too busy a mind or business life can destroy your life and business. I call this principle of space 'the absence of content'. Hom the tea entrepreneur, who was busy travelling the world and managing countless logistics, realized he needed some time 'just to be'. **Too much content leads to discontent.** More often than not the first way I help clients is to simplify their lives. You can't pour more water into a full cup without causing a spillage.

Whatever it is that you do from now on it's wise to leave a little bit of room for you. It is essential that you continue to take yourself back to clarity. Just as furniture needs clearing out from time to time, computers need to have disk space cleared and rooms need clearing, so do you.

All intertwines

As you build your business from your heart, all the themes we've discussed will blend and bind together. The *clarity* you have about who you are and what you do leads you to serve the right *customers*, who can derive value from your services. *Courage* emerges naturally as you follow your heart and run your business in line with your values. *Cooperation* builds with like minds that you seek out and who are drawn to you – and fruitful *conversations* and rich collaboration emerge. You become more connected, resourceful, *creative* and productive. As this happens – and for this to continue to happen – you'll find you become more in tune with yourself and all around. And as this happens *compassion* grows, enriching your life, relationships, services, staff, products and services. From here, you're best placed to embrace, shape and grow from the *change* that will occur throughout your personal and business life.

To me, a legacy is not something that you leave behind when you are gone; it is something that you create while you are here.

This approach to life *now* means you don't wait for some mythical time in the future for your rewards. You should feel that richness each day, in each moment, in each challenge. This whole journey should be rich – sometimes wonderfully rich as you win business, sometimes painfully enriching as you lose a customer and find yourself stretched and you need to find extra clarity, courage, creativity or compassion and have conversations that lead to creativity and collaboration and customers.

As you view life though this lens, even change takes on a differing perspective – it becomes part of the movement of life.

Entrepreneurial evolution

It's time that we exchange the word 'change' for 'evolution'. It's more liberating and insightful, because evolving personally and as a business is necessary to survive, develop and thrive. Rita, the trainer and management consultant who runs change management programmes for major corporations, puts it this way: 'The word "change" suggests that you address it once and it's done. I remind managers that change is ongoing.'

All the business owners featured in this book are evolving in differing ways. Here's how a few of them are evolving:

- ♥ Andy, who wanted to set up a live music night in a bar with his friend, has done so. He found a venue, utilized his network to research his customers, and through it he found a band he's working on collaborating with. He's still doing his day job, so as things evolve he can decide whether it suits him, calculate how financially viable it is and then move into it as a full-time business if it works for all concerned.

♥ Jerome, who has the information technology social media platform business, is adjusting to being manager of a growing business and staff team. They're moving into new premises in India. Month by month he's signing up new colleges and universities. He has been recognized with an award for entrepreneurship by Vellore Institute of Technology, a leading engineering institution in India.

♥ Susan is delegating her virtual assistant work to her associates to focus on helping support her 'expert' clients to raise their profiles. She realizes she needs to be more of a 'lion than a lamb' and raise fees and work with the 'right' clients to boost her income. She's working to complete her guide book for those who want to set up as virtual assistants and plans to run workshops in the future.

♥ Robert's finance and software business and staff team are growing steadily. They too have moved to bigger offices. His teamwork with Neville is working well, and they are attracting major new clients. Their software-product-based business model means there's huge scope for scaling the business and product sales; one company might buy hundreds of licences of one of the products. At the time of writing they were on the verge of signing a major international contract.

Meanwhile Lewis, Donald, Foluke, Nadine, Tom, Karen, Hom, Simon, Tum, Thierry, Liz, David, Jez and the other business owners mentioned in this book are all evolving their businesses in a way that works for them. Some are developing new products and services, forging new business relationships and extending their networks and support to help them progress. For some, like Rita, Hom and Parit, the evolution has also seen their work extend into new countries.

Entrepreneurial evolution takes many shapes and forms and is ongoing. In my own case it has involved starting and closing a business, clarifying what's really important to me, developing tools and products, and learning to balance pursuing my ideas with focusing on ensuring a reliable cash flow. It has involved learning where my magic is and gaining work as a public speaker and a coach to leaders, teachers and healers, including entrepreneurs, chief executives, entertainers, and those on a journey to find their true self and build their life and career on it. I've learnt to hold fast to what works for me as a business owner so that I am available to those who really derive value from my service. I learnt to embrace my mission of helping raise our connectivity, compassion and consciousness. So this book is part of my own evolution, my contribution and the work I'm drawn to do to achieve my mission.

For me it's always about listening closely to my instinct and following it – even if it means I'm the only one walking that path and even if there's no guarantee of it leading anywhere. I do it because it's who I am and because it feels most true to what needs to be done. Every time I've done this I've evolved and made an impact on those I serve. It is the courage to change the entire nature of a speech I have been asked to give when I see it is not the one that is needed.

Sometimes entrepreneurial evolution means letting go, realizing that a business is not for you, doing something else or moving on. Rare is the entrepreneur who hasn't made mistakes, experienced hard times or had business 'failures'. This has been the case in small or big ways for many of the entrepreneurs in this book, and invariably it has been these major hurdles that have led to the greatest insights, shrewdest business decisions and personal growth. If you are an inventor, all of those flawed prototypes hone and help mould the ideal one.

A soul trader has the heart of an athlete. As the old adage goes, people show what they are made of not by how they respond when things go well but how they respond when things don't. What's more, it tends to be the times when we are at a loss, the times when we are in the wilderness, that we wake up, open our eyes and remember what is really important in life and that we live and work from that space. In some cases that evolution means picking ourselves up and dusting ourselves down; in some cases it means changing things around. In some cases – including for some business owners I've met and worked with – it means selling up, packing up and moving on to something else. The important thing is remaining aware and alert. Remember that we change and our circumstances change. It is no different to when we have changed roles, jobs or vocations – sometimes by design, sometimes through external factors. It is the ability to learn, evolve and appreciate that is most important.

10 things that may need to change

Many things may need to change as you move ahead. Here are just 10 such examples of common themes that I have seen as a business coach. Being aware of these may help you spot them and react swiftly:

1 **Mindset:** If you don't believe it you probably won't achieve it (or enjoy it).

2 **Business model/type:** Change it if it's not paying off for you or those you serve.

3 **Team, structure and systems:** An inspired, gifted, organized team will win the league.

4 **Network, associates and suppliers:** You need a rich reservoir that serves all.

5 **Working habits:** The right blend, with attention on marketing, operations and finances.

6 **Certain customers:** If you're not serving them and/or they're not serving you.

7 **Business partners:** Marriages require trust, talking, respect, equity and growth.

8 **Relationships:** At home, at work and in the world, they need to be nourished and nourishing.

9 **Attitude and approach:** A healthy approach to money, people and success is key.

10 **Skill set and style:** Is it time to raise your game or change your ways?

What else might need to change? Are there any things that you feel need changing now? If so, what help and support do you need, and who can help you with that change?

> **TIP** Many businesses spend too much time on admin and not enough on marketing and sales. Whilst admin and operational matters are *doing the business work*, they are not necessarily *bringing in the business*. Operations and admin are like setting and clearing the table. Marketing and sales are shopping and putting food on the table. Only through shopping will you have something to eat and something to clear up after.

Mindful business

Your life and your business will be fulfilling, rich and sustainable when you run them mindfully. The more mindful you are of being clear, appreciating customers, being courageous, working co-operatively, having rich conversations, being compassionate and embracing change, the more wonderful the journey will be.

Too often life and business are all about having a full mind. A full mind is not helpful. It is a weight. It is a burden. It is a hindrance. Mindful business is where compassionate businesses emerge from. Business does not operate in a vacuum. It's part of life and your wider world. The more mindful you are, the more adept you will become, and you'll become and remain more in tune with everyone in your business and home life. Hom the tea entrepreneur puts it this way: 'I can see how the world and business fail when people don't listen to their heart or when business is not *of* the heart.'

I remember working with a charming, successful entrepreneur who runs a design and innovation business. He was at a point of change. He really wanted to look at what to do next in business. He spent time diligently reflecting on his career to date, doing all sorts of personality profiles to check what might suit him, and he explored what his virtual mentors might do. I asked him: 'What is left to create? What if anything do we actually need as a species?' These are the questions for soul traders. This is the invitation for soul traders so that we can remember that the root of invention, innovation, creativity, enterprise, exchange and business is producing things that will serve us.

We are in interesting times, and things are changing. More soul traders are running businesses from the heart. There is a raised consciousness about creating business that does not serve selfish wants but meets real needs.

Transformational business

Business should never be transactional;
it should always be transformational.

If you run your business mindfully, you'll have a remarkable business. It will transform your life and those of the people around you. That transformation may be about moving from a job you hate to creating a business that you love or something far more wide-reaching.

What tips and what advice would your virtual mentors give you? Whenever you come to a point where you feel stuck I invite you to check in with the book and with your virtual and actual mentors and advisers you know, love and trust.

What is it that you could transform in your life and work? Mindful of your mission from Chapter 1, what needs transformation?

- ♥ How can you keep your **clarity**?
- ♥ How can you powerfully connect to and serve your **customers**?
- ♥ How will you maintain your **courage**?
- ♥ What is the kind of **cooperation** you need to seek out and forge now?
- ♥ What **conversations** do you need to have, and which will transform your relationships?

♥ What ways could you be a little more **creative** – and a lot more?

♥ What needs to be accepted and what will you **change**?

Some answers may take weeks or months to emerge. That can be a good thing, because by merely asking the questions and living with them your awareness and insight can expand. In some cases there may be no answers. This realization and acceptance of the changing ways and weather of life and yourself can often be the most powerful kind of transformation.

As you move forward, how will you stay on track? How is it you can build in that time and that space for you? It might be about finding silence each day as I do. It may be a walk in the forest to reconnect and clear your head as it is for Rita. It may be about a practical step like revisiting your business plan.

It's not the world that needs to change.
It's our consciousness we must raise.

As we've touched on, over recent decades there's been a shift within business, organizations and consumer habits: sustainability, reusable energy, social enterprise and ethical business. We're actually talking about changing our mindsets – in order to change our actions and habits in life.

In other words, these worldly issues are created by us – they are essentially 'mind made'. They're born of the way that we look at ourselves, others and the world. The changes mentioned have come about by *raising our consciousness*, and we can raise that consciousness a bit further. By being aware that it is our relationship with our minds that creates the divide and conflicts, we can set about life from a more mindful heart.

We've lifted the veil of business to get to the heart of how you can truly build a business that you and your customers love. This can be attained and sustained genuinely only through clarity, caring about your customers, having courage, cooperating with others, having rich conversations that convert into business, being creative, and being compassionate throughout life and business changes.

As a soul trader you can ask 'What is it that really resonates with me?', 'What is it that we truly need?', 'What would truly enhance people's lives?' and 'What would really help us progress and evolve?'

Moving beyond a limiting mindset is what every great inventor, innovator and entrepreneur has always achieved. They have done it by looking afresh, looking anew, and looking beyond what others see. They have not been limited by conventional thinking. Often thinking has had nothing to do with it. They've been more interested in understanding the mind and freeing themselves from it than merely thinking through it. They have opened up the window of the mind. They have opened the doors of possibility. They have helped us walk into rich new landscapes. As a soul trader you may have the advantage of a more conscious *heart* – let it lead the way.

If your heart isn't in it, why are you?

INDEX